SOBER SAINTS
Should Christians Drink Alcohol?

Keith Malcomson

Second edition October 2013

Copyright © March 2013 Keith Malcomson

All rights reserved.

ISBN:1470165279
ISBN-13:9781470165277

DEDICATION

In memory of my father and grandfather, both now with the Lord, who were both great lovers of alcohol but who were both delivered from it at the point of salvation by the power of Jesus Christ.

CONTENTS

	Introduction	vii
1	Wine in the Bible	Pg 1
2	The Vine and Wine Production	Pg 17
3	Facts About Alcohol	Pg 29
4	Strong Drink	Pg 43
5	Drunkenness	Pg 57
6	Leadership and Alcohol	Pg 69
7	Social Drinking Amongst God's People	Pg 83
8	Sober Saints	Pg 95
9	A Spirit-filled Life	Pg 103
10	Legalism or Liberty	Pg 117
11	Questions and Answers	Pg 127
12	Christ, Wine and Alcohol	Pg 161

KEITH MALCOMSON

INTRODUCTION

This book was written for three types of persons:
1. those who are convinced that it is ok to drink alcohol socially and moderately.
2. those who are fully persuaded that Scripture forbids the drinking of alcohol.
3. those who stand in the middle unsure of the clear teaching of the Bible.

In the following chapters of this book we will deal with the whole subject of alcohol as it relates to social drinking, Church order and Leadership as taught in the Bible, and whether the Word of God encourages or discourages Christians to drink alcohol.

This subject is certainly one of several hotly debated subjects amongst professing born-again believers in this hour. This simple book will challenge many contemporary opinions, traditions, excuses and false teachings. It will expose several well-known, oft repeated, and popular myths which are perpetually passed on from mouth to ear.

It is a practical book for scholars, leaders, mothers, teenagers and all who have an interest, opinion, concern or doubt concerning alcohol and the teaching of the Bible on alcohol. It will answer many questions as well as challenge some strongly held traditions.

I write for the average young believer as well as the mature seasoned believer; the uneducated as well as the theologian; the mother at home as well as the pastor of a church. I want to be understood. I want to face every hard question head-on. I want to give solid scriptural answers which will withstand the passing of time or any change of culture. This book is for all and should be read by every Christian no matter whether they agree or not.

It will equip leaders and preachers with the solid simple facts which will enable them to biblically and persuasively deal with it in their churches and ministries. It will give clear answers to those who have had questions which they could not answer and will settle nagging doubts in their mind. I hope it will be a convincing, persuasive, doctrinal yet gracious challenge to those who have held opinions and convictions moulded by contemporary practice rather than biblical truth.

Alcohol is a contemporary and vital issue that must be faced by the Church in this hour. Over 85% of all adults in our world drink alcohol. In Russia over 40% of men suffer from alcoholism. In North America the devastating and tragic effects of alcohol are very evident and well known amongst native Indians.

Every nation, culture, and country is impacted by alcohol. Even if you do not drink you can be absolutely sure that its influence indirectly affects your life on a daily basis.

But the problem does not stop there. There has been a dramatic rise in social drinking among Christians since the new millennium. This new phase of social drinking has resulted in a steady rise of serious problems which are presently being ignored by the Church of our generation. We are presently sowing the wind but will reap the whirlwind unless a change comes.

For about ten years I had a desire to come aside and study this subject concerning alcohol and the Bible in a full, in-depth manner, but because of ministry responsibilities and more vital pressing needs I never quite found the time. But in November 2009, I finally did find the time.

Before embarking on my quest I searched my heart as to my motives, opinions and convictions as well as to my willingness to submit to all that a thorough and accurate study would reveal even if it utterly changed some precious personal conviction which I had previously held.

I set my heart sincerely toward God to be taught of Him from His Word afresh. Over a period of five days of study questions I had held in my mind for years, were suddenly answered and such clarity and insight came to me on this subject that I was compelled to publish my findings in an online article which drew great interest every month since then.

At that time I had no thought of writing a book for publication. But this led to further months and years of study both of the Bible and of authors both ancient and modern who wrote both for and against the practice of social drinking by Christians. I believed that if what I had found was the truth of

God then it could withstand any argument or question raised up by man's wisdom or scholarship. I was keen to understand clearly every argument from every angle and to faithfully deal with these in the light of God's Word. This book is the end result. It has mostly been written in Ireland although I have studied and written portions in different lands.

Whatever you believe on this subject I would simply ask these three things of you. Firstly, approach what I have written with a *"readiness of mind"*—an open, willing, eager mind—to hear what the Bible teaches. Secondly, *"search the scriptures daily"* on this issue. Study God's Word yourself as you read this book in order to know and understand the mind of God rather than man's opinion (Acts 17:11). Thirdly, please read to the end before drawing your final conclusions. Don't judge what I have written without reading what I have written.

May the Lord bless you, speak to you, lead you, teach you and change you as you read prayerfully, honestly, humbly, sincerely, earnestly and carefully.

Keith Malcomson, March 2013

"I therefore admire those who have adopted an austere life, and who are fond of water, the medicine of temperance, and flee as far as possible from wine, shunning it as they would the danger of fire." **Clement of Alexandria** (150-215)

"If experience gives me a right to advise…I would begin by urging you and warning you, as Christ's spouse, to avoid wine as you would a poison. For wine is the final weapon used by demons against the young." **Jerome** (346-420)

"I had rather be a sober heathen than a drunken Christian." **William Gurnall** (1617-1679)

"You see the wine when it sparkles in the cup, and are going to drink of it. I tell you there is poison in it! and therefore, beg you to throw it away. You answer, 'The wine is harmless in itself.' I reply, Perhaps it is so; but still if it be mixed with what is not harmless, no one in his senses, if he knows it at least, unless he could separate the good from the bad, will once think of drinking it. If you add, 'It is not poison to me, though it be to others'; then I say, Throw it away for thy brother's sake, lest thou embolden him to drink also. Why should thy strength occasion thy weak brother to perish, for who Christ died?" **John Wesley** (1703-1791)

"Next to the preaching of the Gospel, the most necessary thing to be done in England is to induce our people to become abstainers." **C.H. Spurgeon** (1834-1892)

CHAPTER 1
WINE IN THE BIBLE

First and most importantly, as we approach this vital subject, we must realise that when the word *wine* is used in our English Bibles, it is a broad, generic term which includes two different and specific beverages. The first is **grape juice,** which is non-alcoholic or unfermented, and the second is an **alcoholic or fermented drink**, which can intoxicate or make a person drunk.

Those who say that the word *wine* in the Bible always means unfermented grape juice are wrong, but so too are those who say that the word *wine* in the Bible always, and only, means an alcoholic drink.

In fact, no less than thirteen different Hebrew and Greek words are used for our one English word, *wine,* in the Bible. These various Hebrew and Greek words can be broken down into three groupings:

    i)   Those which mean only a fermented drink like *shekar.*

    ii)   Those which only mean an unfermented drink like *tirosh.*

    iii)   And those words which can be used for both like *yayin.*

The fact that we use only one English word to cover thirteen different Greek and Hebrew words should make us cautious about making assumptions regarding wine and alcohol in the Bible. Sadly, too many believers hold dogmatically to opinions without careful, informed study. Furthermore, it is remarkable, and regrettable, that there are a number of contemporary Christian studies written in promotion of the drinking of alcohol which are ignorant of these simple facts or which simply and deliberately ignore them.

A Generic Term

The term *generic* is derived from the word '*genus*' and has the same root as the word 'general'. A *generic* term is one which covers a group of 'things of a kind' and can include two or more, different and even opposite things.

An example of a generic term in our own day is the word *crow*. We may name a black, scavenger bird which appears in our back garden, '*crow*', when in fact the bird is specifically a Jackdaw, belonging to the generic group, 'crows', which includes Ravens, Jackdaws, Magpies and of course the common Rook.

The word *man* as used in the Bible, most times simply means the *male*, but at other times is used in a generic manner to mean *mankind* and is used to cover and include both male and female (Gen.6:3-7; Rom.2:6; 3:4, 28).

We also find that the word *meat,* as used in older English versions of the Bible or older dictionaries and history books, included *all food or nourishment*. We are told that the *'meat'* of John the Baptist was *"locusts and wild honey"* (Mt.3:4). We also read that the leftover's of the bread and fish, which was gathered after Christ's miracle, was called *"meat"* (Mt.15:37). Yet today, if we were to be asked, "Do you eat meat?" we would presume the question referred exclusively to eating 'flesh of an animal'.

I write this to emphasize what has happened to the interpretation of the word *wine* and to reiterate that when we read the word *wine* in our English Bible, we must understand that it is a *generic term*.

The Definition is Altered

Furthermore, we have the issue of 'evolving dictionaries'. In old English dictionaries of the past, *wine* was defined as a generic term for **all drinks produced from the fruit of the vine**, which included both alcoholic wine as well as non-alcoholic grape juice. Sadly, the understanding of most today bears the influence of modern dictionaries and the modern interpretation of wine being synonymous with *alcoholic wine*. This is understandable, but incorrect.

Noah Webster, compiled the first American dictionary. Webster was a master linguist who understood and mastered the meaning of words, their definitions, and the need for accurate and precise word usage in communication.

In the 1828 Webster Dictionary, under the word, *must*, in relation to the fruit of the vine he states: "New wine; wine pressed from the grape but not fermented." Elsewhere in this edition he also shows that *wine* can be a fermented drink **or** sweet juice of some fruit, not just the grape.

Again, in the 1913 International Edition, *must* is defined as: "The expressed juice of the grape, or other fruit, before fermentation." *Wine* is defined as: "The expressed juice of grapes, especially when fermented; a beverage or liquor prepared from grapes by squeezing out their juice and (usually) allowing it to ferment."

These definitions confirm that over a period of almost 100 years in the first American English dictionaries, it was commonly understood that the word *wine* could be used for **'grape juice before, during or after fermentation.'**

By the seventh edition of Webster's dictionary, *wine* is defined as: "Fermented grape juice containing varying percentages of alcohol..." By this time, no room is left for defining wine as unfermented grape juice.

It may be easily proved that from the 17th to the 19th Centuries, secular lexicons and dictionaries defined the word *wine* correctly—as a broad term. However, from the mid-20th Century onward, alteration of the definition has dominated secular and Christian dictionaries.

This has had the regrettable result of confusing many genuine believers who believe that the word *wine* in the Bible always, and only, means a fermented drink. This most basic fact is fundamental in leading multitudes to misunderstand and misrepresent the teaching of the Bible in relation to alcohol.

This simple mistake has also led great multitudes to incorrectly assume that Christ and His disciples drank alcohol. This misconception has been held to and passed on without checking the facts and without thorough study.

Nine Hebrew words are used in the Old Testament, and **four Greek** words in the New Testament for our one English word *"wine"*, and they do not all mean the same thing: some are intoxicating, some are not, and some are generic terms which include both. We will work with just three of these for now: two Hebrew and one Greek.

Yayin

In the Old Testament *yayin* is the most popular term for *wine*, being used 141 times. It is used in 31 of the 39 books of the Old Testament and is used throughout the written history of God's people from the days of Noah to the days of Nehemiah. To grasp the definition of this one word and to understand it correctly, is fundamental to understanding what the Bible teaches about wine.

As we take a quick look at how the term *yayin* is used in the Old Testament, note that it is not just a simple term for alcoholic wine as some presume and promote. It is used in a great variety of ways to mean anything from **grapes hanging on a tree, to wine in a cup.**

Yayin is spoken of as that which is gathered as a harvest prior to going into the winepress, and certainly before the beginning of the fermentation process (Jer.40:10, 12); also while still in the winepress before coming out (Isa.16:10); and again of that which comes forth from the winepress prior to fermentation (Jer.48:32-33). In fact even that which is not as yet gathered but rather destroyed is also called *yayin* (Deut.28:39).

We also see in Genesis 49:11 that *yayin* is not restricted to fermented wine: *"Binding his foal unto the vine, and his ass's colt unto the choice vine..."* A part of Judah's blessing was that the vine would grow in such abundance, that men would tie their foals and asses to them.

"...he washed his garments in wine [**yayin**], *and his clothes in the blood of grapes:"* Typically of Hebrew literature (which often employs such parallelism) the author of Genesis

here paints one picture with two different phrases. He confirms twice over that he who treads out grapes in the winepress, has his garments washed with *yayin* (Isa.63:1-4). The juice which he is treading out under his feet has not had time to ferment and is therefore fresh unfermented wine without any question or doubt. He is very clear in defining this **yayin** as **fresh juice;** *"the blood of grapes."*

Simply put: to limit and restrict *yayin* to meaning *only* fermented wine does not work when tested by the written Scriptures. You cannot, and do not *gather* alcoholic wine from vines at harvest time. Alcoholic wine is fermented not gathered.

We can find in a number of scriptures that corn and wine are basics of life (Gen.14:18; Jdg.19:19; I Sam.10:3; 16:20; II Sam.6:19; 16:1-2; Neh.5:15; Prov.9:5; Ecc.9:7). In **Lamentations 2:12** *yayin*-wine is used to describe the drink which suckling babes cry out for in the midst of terrible famine: *"...the children and the sucklings swoon in the streets of the city. They say to their mothers, Where is corn and wine* **[yayin]***?"* These *'children and sucklings'* were accustomed to *'corn and wine'* for refreshment. But now they are perishing for lack thereof. These babes are still sucking the breast of their mothers but are of such an age as to be able to speak. It is unimaginable that a mother, regardless of culture, would give a suckling babe, alcohol as a drink, even less so when famishing of hunger and thirst. *Yayin* here was the simple juice of the grape which would satisfy, nourish and refresh the child.

On the other hand, *yayin* can mean an intoxicating alcoholic drink. Indeed, where you have the potential of making grape juice, you also have the potential of making alcoholic wine, which is why these two drinks are so closely connected and frequently confused.

We have numbers of examples in the Bible of *yayin* stealing the senses of men and leaving them in a state of drunkenness in which they did not know what they were doing (Gen.9:21, 24; 19:32-35) so, for anyone to imply that Bible wine could not intoxicate is to contradict the written Scriptures. **Genesis 9:21** is very clear when it says that Noah *"drank of the wine* **[yayin]**, *and was drunken;"* the end result of this was a state of unconscious nakedness.

Some bring forth theories that the wine of Bible days was weaker (less alcoholic) than today, or that it was commonly and normally mixed with water and as a result carried a very low amount of alcohol which consequently had very little effect upon the average person. Again a clear study of the Bible will show that this is not correct. It is evident that the fermented wine of the Bible was well-able to make grown men drunk.

Yayin makes no sense if only and always applied as being an unfermented drink and the same is true if only applied as a fermented drink. If exclusive use of either one of these is executed, great inconsistencies and contradictions arise on both sides of the argument.

So we can see clearly that *yayin* is used throughout the Old Testament for grapes on the tree, grapes in the winepress, the juice squeezed out from the press, unfermented wine as well as for fermented wine. To restrict this word to only fermented wine is neither correct nor honest.

In fact the use of the Hebrew word *yayin* is similar to our English use of the word *wine*; both are used broadly for alcoholic and non-alcoholic grape drinks. The only way to discern exactly what is meant when dealing with a generic word in Scripture is to study the **context.** If a particular word has the potential of several different meanings then a study of the context is demanded; is vital and is necessary in order to come to a correct conclusion and accurate interpretation.

When *yayin* is used in Psalm.104:14-15 it is commended, but when the same word is used in Proverbs 20:1 and 23:31, it is condemned. In one place it is considered a blessing, but in another a curse. In one place it is approved, but in the other it is disapproved. In one place it is a means of blessing, and in another, a means of sorrow. In one place it is to be laboured for, expected and sought for, but in another place it is to be shunned, rejected and avoided. In one place it is a symbol of the wrath of God, but in another it is a symbol of the mercy of God.

Robert P. Teachout in his thorough word study says: "half of the times *yayin* occurs in the Old Testament (71 times) the text is talking about grape juice; in the other half of the 141 references, scripture is talking about wine."[1] While we have no desire to be dogmatic about exact numbers or percentages we do point this out as a rough estimate.

The same is true concerning sex and the eating of food in the Bible. The context reveals if the sexual act is according to God's laws and therefore blessed, or if it contradicts God's Word and is condemned as a sinful act. Eating is either condemned as gluttony or commended for strengthening the body, depending on the context.

Yayin *Defined in Jewish Tradition*

Julius (Judah David) Eisenstein (1854–1956), was a Polish-born Jew, who moved to America in 1872. He established America's first society for the Hebrew language and was a fervent lover of the language as well as the customs and practice of this people. He contributed more than 150 entries to the *Jewish Encyclopaedia* (1901–1906) and authored thousands of articles for newspapers, journals and encyclopaedias.

In his article on wine he states: "There were different kinds of wine..." and then goes on to enumerate the various types, kinds and names of wines used by the ancient Jew. Under the term wine he places both fermented and unfermented drinks. He also states: "Fresh wine before fermentation was called *'yayin-mi-gat'* (wine of the vat)." This reveals that *yayin* did not always and only denote a fermented drink in the Jewish mind.

It is important to take good note of such a quote because those who promote the social drinking of alcohol frequently and dogmatically state that no Jewish scholars—ancient or modern—considered unfermented grape juice to be wine. This quote quite obviously exposes this as utterly untrue.

Nehemiah speaks of receiving *"all sorts of wine* [yayin]*"* every ten days while the small remnant rebuilt the walls of Jerusalem (Neh.5:18). This was all different kinds, sorts and manners of wine, proving again that it is a generic term. The nature of the word *yayin* makes it impossible to mean only and always a fermented drink.

---

[1] p.30, *Wine the Biblical Imperative: Total Abstinence*, Robert P. Teachout.

This small remnant of burdened people who worked so hard each day needed constant good strength, alertness and refreshment. Fermented wine would not help this vital work but pure grape juice most certainly would sustain these workers. Nehemiah took heed to Solomon in not allowing his people, soldiers and workers to look at fermented drinks that would hinder the work of revival and restoration.

If only an alcoholic drink was meant by the word *yayin* then why not use the word *shekar* which is the common Hebrew word used distinctly, and exclusively for alcoholic drinks? Obviously the word *shekar* is not sufficient to describe what *yayin* describes.

In conclusion, *yayin* is both encouraged and forbidden in Scripture; it is condemned as an intoxicating drink but encouraged as a non-intoxicating drink. In the first instance, this speaks of fermented wine but in the second of the fresh juice of the grape. The only way to resolve this is to accept the fact that **it is a broad, generic term, understood by its context.**

Tirosh

The second most commonly used word for *"wine"* in the Old Testament is *tirosh*. It is found 38 times, of which 26 times it is translated as *"wine"*, eleven times as *"new wine"*, and one time as *"sweet wine."* It is always spoken of as a blessing and never warned against. It is given as a good, pure, wholesome gift from God.

It is mentioned by 14 different biblical authors over a period of one thousand years yet consistently and without change. This consistent use of the word leaves us in no doubt as to its meaning.

Even those who teach that Christians can drink alcohol freely admit that *tirosh* most often and primarily means fresh grape juice (*must*). So already we see that here is a substance called *"wine"* in the Old Testament which consistently means an unfermented substance. All are agreed. (This one thought alone undermines the myth that the word *"wine"* is always and only a fermented drink.)

Moreover, not once is *tirosh* revealed as a fermented drink in the Bible and most often it is the **fruit** of the grape—not even the juice. There is only one passage in which there is even a possibility that it could be a drink (Isa.62:8-9). But this needs to be proven so let us take a closer look.

We are told that it is found in the grape cluster (Isa.65:8); that it withers and dries up (Isa.24:7; Joel 1:10); is attacked by a drought (Hag.1:11); is gathered (Deut.11:14; Isa.62:9); eaten (Deut.12:17-18); trodden (Mich.6:15); laid up in heaps (II Chron.31:5-6); put in storehouses (32:28) and in just one reference is spoken of as a drink (Isa.62:8-9).

It clearly refers to the grape harvest which contains the juice and may refer to the fresh grape juice produced which is called "new wine." It is always associated with that which is grown in the earth. It is distinct from *yayin* as revealed in Micah 6:15: *"Thou shalt…tread the…sweet wine* [**tirosh**], *but shalt not drink wine* [**yayin**]." Here we see that *tirosh* is trodden in order to produce *yayin* to drink.

Of its 38 references, in 19 of these it is mentioned alongside corn (*dagon*) and olives which produce oil (*yitshar*), which are all produce of the field (Deut.7:13; 11:14; 12:17; 14:23; Neh.10:37; Joel 2:24). A further eleven times it is mentioned with corn and twice more-with oil. In these references we are told that all three are eaten. This means that almost always *tirosh* is associated with the raw harvest produce used to make bread, oil and wine. Only in six out of 38 mentions of *tirosh*, is corn or oil not mentioned together with it.

We must make reference to Judges 9:13 here: *"And the vine said unto them, Should I leave my wine* [**tirosh**], *which cheereth God and man, and go to be promoted over the trees?"*

The misinterpretation of this verse is frequently used to 'prove' that fermented wine *"cheereth"* the heart and by this some imply that getting 'happy' by alcohol consumption is commended by God and acceptable to Him. However, the true meaning of this parable reveals an utterly different source and reason for cheer.

The vine speaks and he actually says 'why would I leave my responsibility in producing "wine" [**tirosh**]', which as we have seen is the **fruit** on the vine, 'and go take another job?' We can clearly see this has nothing to do with drinking alcohol to the point of being happy and God being glad about it. The vine was saying that his production of the vine **harvest** made both God and man happy. It has nothing to do with alcohol, never mind the drinking of it.

Furthermore, God does not have to *"drink"* wine in order to be glad! But lack of context will inevitably result in the misuse of Scripture. This scripture has too often been taken out of its clear context and twisted in order to create a doctrine which says that God takes pleasure in seeing man get happy on alcohol. Again, Julius Eisenstein writing in the *Jewish Encyclopaedia* concerning *tirosh* says "...tirosh includes all kinds of sweet juices and must, and does not include fermented wine."

But what about Hosea 4:11, where it says: *"Whoredom and wine* [yayin] *and new wine* [tirosh] *take away the heart."*? We are told that three things take away the heart in this verse; whoredom, wine and new wine. It is inferred by some that to *"take away the heart"* means intoxication and so it is presumed that *new wine* (tirosh) here must mean fermented wine. Since this is the only single reference that could potentially see *tirosh* understood as an alcoholic drink, and is the only passage in the Old Testament where *tirosh* is used or spoken of in a negative manner, we need to flesh out the context of this verse to add integrity to the preceding presentation on *tirosh*, keeping in mind that in every other reference *tirosh* is considered a blessing from God.

The passage says all three together take away the heart. Whoredom is sexual sin, such as adultery or fornication, or in a spiritual sense, it is idolatry. In the verses surrounding this reference it is clearly talking about Israel going after false gods, in a backslidden condition and of worshipping idols (v6-17).

In verse ten it says, *"they shall eat, and not have enough: they shall commit whoredom, and shall not increase."* One part of their departure was eating. New wine (*tirosh*) would most certainly be a part of this. There are several products of the vine (including food products) that would be part of a feast. Several times in Scripture we are told that overeating (gluttony) can make you forget God. More things take away the heart than fermented wine.

Hosea 3:1 also speaks of the condition of Israel in departing from the Lord: *"who look to other gods, and love flagons of wine."* These flagons of wine (*ashyshah 'enab*) were actually **raison cakes** pressed together and eaten. The overindulgence in the eating of such vine products was no doubt a part of the comfortable lifestyle they had created which led to a departure from God.

Also the term *"take away"* is used about 960 times in the Old Testament yet not once is it associated with drunkenness due to alcohol consumption. Furthermore, it says the *"heart"* is taken away, not the mind. This was not a subduing of the faculties of the mind, but a drawing away of the intentions, desires and choices of the heart.

In Hosea 4:11 it is certainly likely that the generic term *yayin* may mean fermented wine for it is used in such a way elsewhere, whereas *tirosh* is never used in any other reference for a fermented drink. To assume it means a fermented, intoxicating drink here would contradict all that we know about it elsewhere in the Scriptures.

Once again and in closing this Hebrew word *tirosh*, clearly refers to the grape harvest and may refer to the fresh grape juice or product of the grape.

Oinos

When we come to the Greek New Testament the most prominent word used for wine is *oinos*. It is used 33 times and is translated as *wine* each time in our English Bibles. The fact that it is used by Christ, in reference to Christ, and by the early church leaders and writers, shows its importance to our discussion.

Although there are four different Greek words in our New Testament translated as the English word wine, *oinos*, outnumbers the others *four to one*. This is why it is important to understand this word above others when we look at wine in the New Testament.

If we look at the use of this Greek word *oinos*, in the secular writings of ancient authors from the Greco-Roman world, we will find that they clearly understood that *oinos* can mean alcoholic wine as well as unfermented wine.

Pliny, Columella, Cato, Polybius and others used this term *oinos* and clearly understood that it could mean simple grape juice just as much as it could mean alcoholic wine. The Greek philosopher Aristotle says: "sweet wine [oinos] would not intoxicate." If *oinos* was only and always alcoholic, Aristotle could never have said this.

To misunderstand this word is to misunderstand the whole New Testament teaching on wine in relation to the Church. Although it seems obvious that it is a generic term for both fermented and unfermented wine, (especially as it is synonymous with *yayin*) we must still take a look at how it is used in the New Testament.

Oinos occurs 33 times in the New Testament. Of these we find that the first ten times that it is used is by Christ in reference to wineskins (Lk.5:37-39; Mk.2:22; Mt.9:17). In these references He talks about *"new wine."* In the Old Testament we saw that *"new wine"* (*tirosh*) was a fresh, unfermented vine harvest or the fresh juice. To be 'new' implies it has been freshly pressed.

Christ uses the distinction between *"new wine"* being put into *"new wineskins"* and contrasts it with *"old wine"* and *"old wineskins."* He was using this practical, cultural, daily custom to draw out in a parable a distinction between the system of the Pharisees and that of His own new Disciples.

The Pharisees had begun as a spiritual movement centuries before with a pure motive, pure message and pure zeal. Now, as a movement, their doctrine had been *leavened* and they had become an old wineskin and useless to God's purpose. They once held the new wine of God but that was long gone.

The new wineskin made out of Christ's Disciples is contrasted with the old wineskin of the Pharisees. The new wine of the gospel being poured into Christ's Disciples is here contrasted with the old legalistic fermented wine of the Pharisees.

Most agree here that the *"new wine"* freshly pressed from the grape and ready to go into the wineskin was unfermented wine. So, straightway we see that Christ and the first Disciples had access to a wine that was fresh and unfermented and Christ used it as an example of His gospel.

If this new wine is put into a new wineskin which is free from previous use, it will be fine and both will be preserved. But if new wine (unfermented) goes into old wineskins it is guaranteed to be lost. An old wineskin would very likely contain ferment (leaven) especially if it had previously contained old fermented wine. This leaven would then initiate the fermentation process in the new wine.

If this new wine was in fact already fermented, or almost fully fermented as some imply, it could have safely been placed in old wineskins without loss. It would not have needed a new wineskin. New wine is put in a new wineskin in order to preserve it from fermentation in order to have a refreshing drink.

New wine is not put in new wineskins in order to ferment. It is a simple fact that a new skin would burst if it held wine during the process of fermentation. (This will be further explained in the answer to questions in chapter 11.)

The gospel is represented in this parable as fresh unfermented wine but the legalistic teachings of the Pharisees are represented by old fermented wine.

By this Christ was rejecting *both* fermented wine and the old legalistic teachings of the Pharisees. His Disciples must not be mixed up with that system. They are utterly distinct in character, purpose and influence. They are to be as different from the system of the Pharisees as new wine is from alcoholic wine.

In Matthew 5:39, He finishes with the following: *"No man also having drunk old wine straightway desireth new: for he saith, The old is better."* A man who has gained a taste, desire and the habit of drinking old, fermented wine does not straightway desire fresh unfermented wine. Fermented wine is addictive. It has a strong influence on the senses and creates dependence. It is much easier (and safer) to simply train new believers to drink *new wine* than it is to train those accustomed to the old fermented wine of the Pharisees, to drink fresh grape juice. Jesus knew what he was talking about.

Christ draws clear distinctions here between wine which is new and that which is old. Both are called wine, both are from the vine, both are produced in the same culture and in the same generation but both are not at all the same. **These two types of wine are as different as the Pharisees and His own Disciples.**

While it is clear that *oinos* is a generic term including freshly pressed unfermented wine it also includes a wine that intoxicates. Paul writes: *"be not drunk with wine (oinos)"* (Eph.5:18). *Oinos,* **when fermented** had the ability to intoxicate. The fermented wine of the New Testament was not weak or watery. It had the ability to relax the inhibitions of any strong man and to make him drunk.

The intoxicating influence of wine is used in a figurative sense in the *Book of Revelation* when talking about Babylon in two different ways. Firstly, concerning the literal city of Babylon (14:8; 18:3), and secondly, concerning the religious system of Babylon (17:2). This city and system holds a cup in her hand that has the power to intoxicate nations (Jer.51:7).

While the true church holds forth a cup of communion filled with the new, pure, unfermented fruit of the vine, this false harlot church in contrast holds forth a cup full of intoxicating wine which makes the nations drunk. This intoxicating wine leads to fornication, idolatry, superstition and false worship. This cup is the reason for God's wrath coming on Babylon and also upon all nations who partake of her wine.

A third sense in which the word *oinos* is used in the *Book of Revelation* concerns the cup of the Lord which is filled with the wine of His indignation and wrath which He pours out upon her and all those associated with her (14:10; 16:19). Fermented wine is undoubtedly meant in these verses and is a fitting picture for a false gospel and world system which is poisonous and deadly and which is set in opposition to the kingdom of God on Earth. It is also a very fitting picture of God's fierce, undiluted and all consuming wrath. All three ways in which it is used by John reveal intoxication through wine leading to destruction.

During the ministry of Christ, and later in the ministry of Peter and the apostle Paul to the gentile churches, we see that drunkenness was a live issue and a serious danger to all. Wine if fermented could send a man to Hell, but if fresh and free from ferment was encouraged and blessed. Both of these drinks were readily available during the First Century in Jerusalem, Judea and across the whole Roman Empire.

CHAPTER 2
THE VINE AND WINE PRODUCTION

No one could possibly doubt the importance of the vine, vineyards and wine in both the Old and New Testaments. Vines are mentioned 54 times and vineyards 94 times in the Old Testament alone. They occur in each of its books with the exception of the book of *Jonah*. The vine is mentioned more in the Bible than any other plant or tree.

While most limit the usefulness and produce of the vine to the production of a fermented drink, the Bible and eastern custom give it a place of great usefulness and even look upon it as a necessity of life.

The vine generally grows on hillsides and in places that other crops could not grow. The vine is highly valued for shade, the fresh fruit of its grapes, for raisons and for vinegar. Its leaves were frequently eaten by cattle and even used by people to stop bleeding or to heal inflammation of the skin. There are also a variety of jams, syrups, jellies, honeys and juices which may be produced from its fruit and even grape oil from its seeds.

It is no wonder then that it was fundamental to the economic condition of the nation of Israel throughout its long history. If there was any failure in the three harvests of wheat, olive and grapes, it was disastrous for the nation. But when it was harvested successfully, it was considered a great gift and blessing from the Lord.

It was specifically created by God with its wide range of physical and nutritious benefits for man's health, blessing and enjoyment. The only product of the vine that is strongly warned against in the Bible is the fermented juice of the grape called wine. No other product of the vine is spoken of as a danger to the physical, mental, moral and spiritual good of man. Of course, *unfermented* wine stands with all the other products as a blessing.

One other use, for which God has created and given the vine and its products is as a tool to bring spiritual instruction and insight to His people. It was and is a precious aid-memoir for divine revelation.

Noah and God's People

Archaeologists, historians, theologians and experts of viniculture are all in agreement that the earliest physical evidence of the cultivation of vines for wine production was strictly within the region of the Fertile Crescent in the ancient Near East reaching from the Caucasus Mountains in the north to ancient Babylonia to the south.

This area also falls between the Mediterranean Sea, the Black Sea and the Caspian Sea. This covers the area of present day Turkey, Armenia and Georgia in the north, as well as northern Iraq and Iran to the south.

The prominent feature of this area is Mount Ararat in the north where Noah's ark came to rest after the worldwide flood of God's judgement more than 1,600 years after creation (about, 2348 BC). It was probably somewhere south of Ararat that Noah and his family initially settled for a time during which Noah first cultivated the vine.

One of the main regions where the earliest physical signs of wine manufacture have been unearthed by Archaeologists is in the Tarsus Mountains of eastern Turkey, which is south-west of Ararat.

It is worthy of note that the most ancient find by archaeologists of six, nine-litre wine jars used in wine production, was at Hajji Firuz Tepe in the northern region of the Zagros Mountains, western Iran, just south of Ararat.

In January, 2011, the oldest relatively complete wine production facility was discovered which included its winepress, vats, storage jars, grape seeds, withered grape vines, remains of pressed grapes, a cup and a drinking bowl in a cave in south east Armenia just 60 miles north of Ararat. All of this is to be expected since Scripture is so clear concerning the first production and use of wine in recorded history which was just prior to the raising up of the first civilisation (Cities) on the plains of Shinar just south of this region.

The first mention of wine in the Bible is found in Genesis 9:21. In the previous verse the vineyard is mentioned for the first time: *"Noah began to be an husbandman, and he planted a vineyard:"* He *"began"* to be a farmer or worker of the ground so it seems that he had not previously been one.

On this occasion we also have the first mention of a man drinking wine and becoming drunk. We not only have much instruction on the blessing of the vine, the vineyard and of wine in the Bible but from its first mention we receive a serious warning through the example of Noah, revealing the curse, heartache and trouble which may arise from its abuse.

After this as the family and descendents of Noah grew and multiplied in number we are told that they moved out in search of a new place to live: *"as they journeyed from the east, they found a plain in the land of Shinar; and they dwelt there"* (Gen.11:2). Shinar (Sumer) is the ancient land of those who first settled in the lower plain between the Tigris and Euphrates rivers. From this we see that the region between Ararat and Shinar is the biblical home of the cultivated vine.

Noah was the first person in recorded history who cultivated the vine in order to produce wine as a drink. Through his sons and their growing families this knowledge of vine cultivation spread as they populated this region known to Historians as the *Cradle of Civilisation*.

After the destruction of the tower of Babel (about, 2242 BC) and the separation of peoples and families through the diversifying of their tongues, vine cultivation spread out from this narrow fertile region into other regions of the world.

Today language experts recognise this region as the "most ethnically diverse and linguistically rich area in the world."[2] The word wine in a host of diverse languages is accepted as a very ancient term and is revealed as such by its similarity right across the diverse language spectrum.

In the ancient language of the Hittites it was called *wiyana;* in Latin it is *vinum;* in Italian it is *vino;* in French and Icelandic it is *vin;* in Old Irish it is *fin;* in Gaelic *fion;* in Welsh *gwin;* in Ethiopian *wain;* in German *wein* and in Russian *vino*. Language experts trace the origin of contemporary languages back to this homeland of the vine.

Even secular vine and wine experts speak of the '*Noah Hypothesis*'. By this they mean the theory concerning the source or beginning of the cultivation of the vine in producing wine. This is the actual name given very aptly by secular scholars to the origin of the vine and wine culture.

Those who teach the '*Noah Hypothesis*' speak of an initial single wild vine which was taken, cultivated, domesticated and used on such a popular scale that today it is still the dominant one. This particular vine is called the *Eurasian Vine* (*Vitis vinifera* L. ssp *sylvestris*).

This particular species (variety) is the source of 99 percent of the world's wine in our own day and is central to any secular history of wine. This very successful species contains a dramatic array of varied sizes, colours, smells and tastes contained in its genes and manifest in its fruit.

Wild grape vines (*Vitis sylvestris*) have separate male and female parts growing on separate vines. The domesticated vine has both male and female parts on the same vine. This *Eurasian Vine* goes back to very ancient days and to a particular vine and vinedresser who deliberately cultivated it and whom we know to be Noah.

Noah chose two wild vines, a male and a female, cultivated them, and made the one original ancestor-vine which we now know as the *Eurasian Vine*. It has no competitor. It stretches from Spain in the west, to central Asia in the east, a

---

[2] p.31, *Ancient Wine*, Patrick E. McGovern

distance of 6,000 kilometres, and from Crimea in the north, to northern Africa in the south a distance of 1,300 kilometres.

From its original home near Ararat the *Eurasian Vine* was transplanted to other areas and was soon cultivated and growing throughout the Near East then the Middle East, including the Jordan valley and Palestine (Canaan) which was an ideal place and climate to grow the vine.

The land of promise (Canaan) was already an effective and fruitful place for vines, vineyards and wine production when Israel arrived there. This land with its climate and geography was perfect for the vine. Many hundreds of ancient winepresses have been discovered across the land which pre-date Israel's arrival.

God's People

In Genesis, as the Lord begins to separate out from the nations a family who will become a great people who will inherit and inhabit the promised land, we read of Abraham receiving bread and wine from the hand of Melchizedek (Gen.14:18). This foreshadows Christ bringing forth provision for His people in these emblems of bread and wine.

Abraham, Isaac, and Jacob dwelt in tents together and we can be assured that they were no strangers to the refreshing fruit of the vine (Heb.11:8-9). When Isaac was old and came to the time for blessing his oldest son Esau he was deceived by the reluctant Jacob who brought him savoury meat and bread to eat as well as wine (*yayin*) to drink (Gen.27:17, 25).

In blessing him Isaac said: *"Therefore God give thee of the dew of heaven, and the fatness of the earth, and plenty of corn and wine* [tirosh]*"* (Gen.27:28, 37). Some try to insinuate that the old man was drunk at this time, but the Bible reveals that he had all his mental faculties about him and that he acted by faith *"concerning things to come"* (Heb.11:20).

The blessing Jacob was blessed with was the product of the field, *tirosh,* which was the fruit of the vine both to eat and to drink as fresh unfermented wine. The blessing is clearly an unfermented drink, not alcohol.

When the Chief Butler sat in the prison with Joseph and the Baker, we read of his dream concerning Pharaoh, which

Joseph interpreted. In it he says: *"And Pharaoh's cup was in my hand: and I took the grapes, and pressed them into Pharaoh's cup, and I gave the cup into Pharaoh's hand"* (Gen.40:11). This reveals a normal custom of producing an unfermented grape juice for the Pharaoh of Egypt.

In Jacob's latter days when he came to bless his sons and to prophesy over them, he speaks of Joseph as *"a fruitful bough, even a fruitful bough by a well; whose branches run over the wall:"* (49:22). Many believe that Joseph is here pictured as a vine. Jacob goes on to say that Joseph would be blessed in a greater way than Abraham, Isaac or Jacob which no doubt included the blessings contained in the vine (25-26).

When we read the song of Moses in Deuteronomy chapter 32, we read of the numbers of blessings with which the Lord blessed the descendents of Jacob including all those connected to harvest as well as livestock. He then finishes with *"thou didst drink the pure blood of the grape"* (32:14). This was the fresh unfermented juice of the grape. This was the drink with which the Lord blessed Jacob and his people down through the generations.

Not once do we read in Israel's history of *"strong drink"* (clearly alcoholic) being a blessing to God's people. Neither is there any evidence that fermented wine was a blessing and a drink commended by God. But many times we are told of the blessing of *tirosh* as well as the *"blood of the grape."*

When the Lord brought Israel to the Promised Land after their forty-year sojourn in the Wilderness under the leadership of Moses and Joshua, the ten spies brought back a token of one cluster of grapes from the brook of Eshcol, near Hebron, which was so large that two men had to carry it between them on a staff upon their shoulders (Num.13:23). This was to become the prominent symbol for Israel as a nation. During the 400 years between the Old and New Testaments, the Maccabees put it on minted coins and in the days of Christ, King Herod's Temple was adorned with a golden vine.

Cultivation of the Vine
Isaiah speaks of the process of establishing a vineyard. A hillside was chosen, the area was fenced, stones were gathered out of the

ground, a choice vine was planted, and a watchtower was built along with a winepress (5:1-7). The exact same process was explained by Christ several hundred years later in one of His parables and in fact vineyards feature in three of His parables (Mt.21:33-34; 20:1: 21:28).

Wild animals, especially foxes, had to be guarded against (Song.2:15) as well as thieves who would come in the night (Jer.49:9). All of this reveals that the cultivation of vineyards involved long hard labour in order to produce a good harvest. It is a gift from God but demands intensive human labour.

The vine demands much care all the year round if it is to prosper and if it is to produce effectively and fruitfully. The vine itself is very vulnerable to all external influences such as cold weather, floods, pests and diseases.

The conditions and environment surrounding the vine and which work upon it as it grows, will greatly affect the colour, size, taste, smell and fruitfulness of the grapes. The three necessities for growing the vine are: heat, sunlight and water.

Ideally grapes should be harvested when the local temperature is 15°C to 21°C (59°F–70°F) and this naturally affects in what regions of the world vines can grow. The grape will not ripen when there is a lack of heat or it will be damaged if scorched by the sun or hot winds. Sunlight is essential in creating the sugar content in the growing grape which is either preserved in unfermented wine or converted to alcohol in fermented wine.

Light frequent rains are essential but heavy rain is destructive. If the ground is too damp the roots may rot, yet the fruit of the vine contains 80% water so on the other hand the vine is utterly dependent upon water. Ancient Israel relied greatly upon the rain coming in its right season for the success of the grape harvest.

Hail showers can destroy a crop at the eleventh hour of production. Light breezes and winds aid the crop but strong winds can rip and damage the crop. A sharp frost can utterly destroy or at least badly damage the crop.

Even the quality of the ground in which it grows is vital. Whether the ground is soft or hard, dark or light, rich in nutrients or lacking in them can alter the final taste of the wine.

The most important task in winter is pruning. Pruning, an ancient art, makes for greater fruitfulness at harvest time. No wonder then that Christ spoke of and used pruning as a spiritual parallel (Jn.15:1-2; Lev.25:4; Isa.5:6; 18:5).

The best vineyards in the world today are those with the best management who carefully watch over every stage of production with skill, patience and strategy. The best wine producers are the best thinkers who give diligent thought, concern and care to the whole process. A good harvest does not come without much work and wine does not make itself on the branch.

When wine producers talk about "vintage" they mean the wine produced from the grapes harvested from the same crop in a particular year. Certain years are good whilst other years are a failure. A certain set of circumstances or change in the weather can almost destroy the harvest.

Even at the point of harvest any good wine producer will tell you that it takes great skill to take good grapes and turn them into good wine. The whole process is again fraught with difficulties and is a careful and complex process.

Although the Bible speaks about the grape harvest, the vineyards and the treading of the grape, it is totally silent about the preparation, preservation, fermentation, storage and commerce of wine, but the same principles and processes operate today as they did in Bible days.

Processing the Grape

When grape juice is initially squeezed out, it has a high content of sugar and is not naturally alcoholic. It is only under the right conditions that yeast cells which are held on the surface of the grape skin or in the surrounding environment begin to act on the sugar content in the grape that the process of fermentation begins, which will eventually turn the grape juice into an alcoholic drink.

As we have already stated, the production of alcoholic wine is a manufacturing business of great skill and always has been. Good alcoholic wine does not develop or create itself; it must be carefully watched over, monitored and engineered. This process of fermentation can fail to begin or can be greatly hindered by too much heat, cold or a number of other conditions. The yeast that ferments the wine is nothing more than a mould or fungus contained either on the skin or in the environment. Fermented wine is frequently made without contact with the skin so the skin is not the vital element.

All moulds do not produce wine. Some bacteria if allowed to work upon the freshly squeezed grape-juice will produce vinegar. Only under very particular conditions and on extremely infrequent occasions will grapes ferment on the vine. It is not a natural or inevitable occurrence.

The most expert wine producers would never consider that fermentation begins on the vine and neither would they assume that it initiates immediately after harvesting. Even after being pressed, fermentation is still held at bay until the grapes and their juice are in the tank where fermentation normally begins.

One expert wine producer states: "We can regulate the fermentation temperature in each tank according to the fruit. We allow *Cabernet Sauvignon* to begin fermentation straight away, but with *Syrah*, we'll chill down the must and give the skins a few days of cold soak before fermentation starts."[3]

Fermentation can be manipulated, retarded, started and prevented. Simon Woods, author of various books on wine and its production as well as a regular contributor to *Wine Magazine* states: "Yeasts won't work below 10°C, and are killed by temperatures greater than 45°C, but it's possible for fermentation to proceed at any point between these two extremes...winemakers often have to heat their cellars in order to kick the fermentation process off at all."[4]

This is a far cry from the opinions of Kenneth L. Gentry who presumes to know better than the experts. When writing in favour of social drinking he says: "...the various instructions from the ancients do not prevent fermentation...fermentation

---

[3] p.93, *Vine to Bottle: How Wine is Made* by Simon Woods, 2001
[4] p.96-97 Ibid

starts the moment the skin is broken, the moment the juice comes forth. Absent [apart from] pasteurization, fermentation is unavoidable." [5]

While the Christian armchair theologians, who promote social drinking, say fermentation is unavoidable the hands-on experts who work in the vineyards and who make their money from it, insist that prevention of fermentation is most certainly possible by using simple methods which the ancients also used.

From this we see that the authors who promote social-drinking promote theories and insist upon ideas concerning fermentation with which secular wine producers and experts clearly disagree. In their desire to justify drinking alcohol they depart from the facts of wine production.

The temperature of wine must be maintained between 18°C and 24°C (65°F and 75°F) in order to produce alcoholic wine. If this procedure is not carried out correctly it can destroy the process of producing alcoholic wine or halt it at a very low alcoholic level.

With hard work wine producers can produce a 14% alcoholic content in the wine, but more normally the end result is 10-12%. Once all the sugar has been turned into alcohol, the process of fermentation ceases. There is no alcohol in grape juice and there is no sugar in alcohol.

If during the fermentation process the temperature of the wine is kept at 45°C (113°F) for about one hour, it will kill the yeasts that produce alcohol. If this was increased to 60°C (140°F) it would kill the whole process in ten minutes.

In the ancient world, during the Old and New Testament period, the production of unfermented wine—free from alcohol—was widespread across the whole Mediterranean world. It was well known and practised. The use of heat, cold, thickening and filtering ensured this process.

Boiling ensured there was no fermentation as it killed the yeasts but concentrated the sugar content as the water evaporated. Fermentation was also prevented by storing it in a cool atmosphere in earthen, airtight vessels. Such grape juice (or

---

[5] p.54, *God Gave Wine* by Kenneth L. Gentry, 2001,

must) could easily be stored for up to two years without fermenting.

Many ancient writers like Virgil, Pliny, Aristotle, Homer and others, wrote concerning the production of wine, both alcoholic and non-alcoholic. They were very clear in explaining in great detail that non-alcoholic wine was widely used all the year round just as they were clear that there was also the means to produce good alcoholic wine for intoxication.

Initial Conclusions

Why have we looked at wine production in this chapter and what does it have to do with the issue of wine and alcohol, and whether a Christian should drink alcohol or not?

We saw clearly in Chapter One, that the word *"wine"* in the Bible does not always mean a fermented drink yet those who promote and teach the social drinking of alcohol militantly and persistently deny that ancient cultures had the ability and knowledge to prevent fermentation of the grapes, and insist that they did not know how to preserve such for extended periods.

Social-drinking defenders would have us believe that the fermentation of the juice of grapes is inevitable and without any possibility of prevention. Some would even have us believe that fermentation begins on the branch and that fermented wine almost comes ready-made from the fruit. This is an utter fallacy.

What is presented in this chapter factually undermines these myths which are foundational to the social-drinking theory.

Experts in the wine business have noted the distinct difference between natural grape juice, which is the fruit of the vine, and that of fermented wine. They are two distinct drinks, separated by the fermentation process, and each produces very different effects upon the human frame.

This myth that there is only one wine in the Bible, and that it is always fermented, is called the "one-wine" theory. The Bible, the ancient writings of secular history, the English language and the facts of the wine industry all agree in revealing them for what they are. Sadly, these myths have gone unchallenged in recent decades which has had a widespread impact upon our present generation, and as a result social drinking has prospered and spread in the Church.[6]

Also, it is repeatedly stated that alcohol (fermented wine) is a gift from God and is a blessing for man whereas the Scriptures show us that it is the vine, its fruit and its fresh juice which is a gift and blessing from God not alcohol or any fermented drink.

I believe that the contemporary teaching that *"wine"* is always and only an alcoholic drink in the Bible may well be one of the most popular myths of our day, and is vital and foundational to the whole theory of social drinking.

---

[6] For those who wish to make a more in-depth study of this subject concerning what these ancient Greek and Roman authors reveal about the production and preservation of unfermented wines, as well as a more comprehensive biblical word study, can find book titles listed in the *Select Bibliography* which will help you.

CHAPTER 3
FACTS ABOUT ALCOHOL

It is a scientific, legal and medical fact that **even the smallest amount** of alcohol affects speech, balance and a person's ability to make clear judgments and decisions. At first this may not be noticeable to the person concerned or obvious to onlookers, however as more alcohol is consumed it becomes noticeable to all.

By the time someone realizes that their alcoholic intake is beginning to affect them it already has. Even after one glass of wine, or one pint of beer, the individual's ability to discern its effect upon themselves has already diminished.

The pathway to drunkenness begins with one drink and the effect is almost immediate with the very first intake. This is true even if the effect is totally unnoticed by all. Medical science tells us that the effect of alcohol reaches the brain within one minute of consumption.

Every part and member of the body is controlled by the brain so anything that affects the function of the brain, affects every part of the body. Alcohol does not need time to digest like food does; it gets VIP treatment and quick access to each member of the body.

When taken, alcohol passes from the stomach into the small intestine, where it is rapidly absorbed into the blood. As a result it can be detected in the blood within three minutes of the first intake. By means of the blood it is then distributed throughout the whole body. Because it is distributed so quickly and thoroughly, the alcohol can affect the central nervous system even in small concentrations.

The liver is capable of breaking down the equivalent of approximately one drink per hour. Until the liver has time to break down the alcohol, it keeps circulating in the bloodstream affecting all of the body's organs, including the brain. The alcohol is then broken down by the liver and finally eliminated from the body.

Alcohol is not a stimulant but a **depressant**. Alcohol depresses the brain and slows down its ability to control the body as well as all its various normal functions. This is why alcohol can be so dangerous. Alcohol acts like a sedative on the brain and as a result slows down muscle coordination, reflexes, movement and speech.

Within the alcohol is the power and ability to undermine the natural God-given abilities of thought and action. The alcohol's first target is the front lobe of the brain which is the area that controls every form of wise judgement and social interaction. Even a small amount of alcohol immediately begins to alter the function of the mind.

Alcohol literally suppresses self-control and natural inhibitions even when taken in low concentrations. Under moderate influence an individual will begin to act differently. It has been more than proven that even an initial drink begins to change the ability of the mind to perceive correctly, to learn or to remember things.

The brain is the organ most affected by alcohol—more than any other member or function of the human body. Of course the fact that alcohol immediately causes decreased reaction time, impaired judgement and impaired memory should at least raise a serious concern in the mind of every genuine believer.

The only reason that someone feels more relaxed, free from stress and anxiety, or happy after a drink is because the alcohol has begun to affect the natural function of the brain by beginning to render God-given faculties out of action. Therefore, alcohol cannot be a gift from God as it works against that which God has given to man.

To say that God would grant and allow man a drink that numbs and dulls his faculties, inducing a joy that is artificial is nonsense. To believe that the Lord would encourage men to hide from troubles, stresses and anxieties in a false counterfeit happiness in which the realities of life are not faced, is a long way from the biblical teaching of how a Christian is to respond to troubles and stresses.

Alcohol also affects the ability to follow objects with the eye; intellectual activities such as arithmetic, memory in storing and retrieving information, the ability to discriminate correctly and attention to detail. All of these things are impaired by a moderate consumption of alcohol.

Research has proven that there is a **5 to15% decrease in response time** after drinking just minimal amounts of alcohol (0.03 % alcohol in bloodstream). This is indeed serious when we take note that the legal limit in the United States and the United Kingdom is 0.08% (80mg), in Germany and France is 0.05% (50mg), and in Norway and Sweden is 0.02% (20mg). This means that in most countries you can drive within the legal limit yet with a greatly lowered response time.

This has also been repeatedly confirmed by various researchers who have recorded this kind of decrease in response time. One such test was carried out on young trainee doctors. They took two separate medical tests but before one of them they drank one glass of wine. All of them thought they had performed better on that particular test but all of them had in fact done far worse. The same happened in the rate of accuracy by typists after just one drink, and young drivers in their reaction/reflex time. All of these tests revealed a dramatic drop in the normal skills of individuals who were not at all aware of it after just one drink.

A few minutes after beginning to drink alcohol almost all cells in the human body are already being influenced to a minor degree albeit unnoticed. It is impossible to take alcohol without such an influence being exerted. As the amount of alcohol taken is increased this influence increases and is manifest. It usually takes a few drinks for the average person to begin to show outward signs of alcohol influence but this is not the beginning of influence.

Although it is popular to consider drunkenness as a state of being "under the influence" of alcohol, in actuality its influence is there in the first sip, drink, glass and pint. **Alcohol is an influence.** You cannot use it without its influence coming to bear on your physical body and mind.

Medical
The best secular advice by the *British National Council of Alcohol*, says that "If you do choose to drink, sip each drink slowly, and always consume alcohol with food. Space drinks out, to no more than one drink per hour, and consume plenty of water in between drinks. Never drink while pregnant and never drive when intoxicated."

Again *The British Dietetic Association* says, "Even a moderate amount of alcohol produces a range of negative short-term effects on the body…" Even the medical world realises that alcohol is a very dangerous drug which must be handled with extreme care. Sadly, many so-called Christians deliberately overstep even this basic worldly wisdom.

Social drinkers who binge can get irregular heartbeats from their alcoholic intake. If any individual drinks too much alcohol, his or her breathing or heart rate can reach dangerously low levels or even stop.

The dangers of excessive drinking range from small short term problems to large terminal problems. Dehydration, dulled senses, weight gain, heart disease, kidney disease, liver disease, blood conditions, loss of long term memory, heart problems, premature dementia and loss of bladder control are all very real dangers.

Half of those diagnosed with cancer in the oesophagus, larynx and mouth are linked to alcohol. Various forms of arthritis can be advanced by alcohol abuse. The list is endless. When consumed in large amounts over a prolonged period of time, alcohol can and will harm virtually every part of your body.

Most medical advice will strongly suggest that pregnant women stay totally clear of all alcohol during pregnancy. The reason for this is that the alcohol travels rapidly through the bloodstream, to the placenta, and directly to the baby.

The baby cannot process the alcohol as fast as the mother can, as its liver is one of the last organs to develop fully and does not mature until the latter half of pregnancy, so the baby is exposed to greater amounts of alcohol for longer periods than the mother which can seriously affect the baby's development.

Alcohol in a foetus has a toxic effect on developing cells and organs, especially in the brain, where it kills cells. Too much alcohol during pregnancy can change the way a baby's face, organs and brain develops. It can also affect the nervous system, which is why learning difficulties and life-long problems with movement and coordination often result.

Miscarriage and premature birth are also a very real danger. Thousands of women each year in all of our nations lose babies because of consuming alcohol before and during their pregnancy, and this trend is increasing. Children damaged during pregnancy may be born small and remain small all their life.

The problems are numerous. This drug endangers the life of humanity on all fronts. As medical science and technology advances, further discoveries concerning the dangers of alcohol to the human body are coming to light. By use of CAT scans (Computed Axial Tomography) the brain can be examined and studied by three-dimensional X-rays. By this means, any damage to brain cells in the frontal lobes of the brain can be gauged.

These new studies have now revealed that even a regular social drinker who has never been intoxicated in his life does damage to his brain cells. These cells are not repaired nor replaced. Similar studies reveal brain shrinkage in those who would be thought light or moderate drinkers.

Such discoveries ought to cause Christians who drink alcohol moderately, socially or occasionally, to rethink what they are doing and participating in. Moderation in drinking alcohol is not the safe alternative that it is made out to be.

The physical body of a believer is the temple of the Holy Spirit. A believer is no longer owner of his body with the right to use it as he will. Christ has redeemed and purchased our bodies by His own blood. We are warned that if any many *"defile"* (shrivel; wither; ruin or corrupt) this temple of God, then God will destroy him (I Cor.3:16-17; 6:19-20; II Cor.6:16; Rom.12:1: I Cor.9:27).

Criminal & Social

Other deadly effects of alcohol upon society are the crime rate and many social problems in our nations.

Whilst writing this chapter, I caught a brief news item informing us that half of those arrested for criminal activity in my own country of Northern Ireland, were under the influence of alcohol.

Again the daily newspaper the, *Irish Examiner*, in September 2010 carried a story entitled '100 People Dying a Month in Alcohol Epidemic.' The facts in the article were taken from a speech by the Irish Government's Chief Medical Officer, of the Department for Health at the time, Dr Tony Holohan. He listed the following damaging effects of alcohol:

> "Alcohol can cause a wide range of family problems from marital breakdown to child abuse and domestic violence. Children of alcoholic parents can suffer the effects of alcohol throughout their lives. Alcohol leads to loss of work, productivity and absenteeism and is associated with crime...More than four times as many people die from alcohol than all other drugs combined. One in four deaths involve males aged 15-34 were caused by alcohol, compared to one in 25 being due to cancer. Suicide rates have doubled in Ireland in the last 20 years. Half of suicides by young males were due to alcohol. One in six child abuse cases were attributed to alcohol. Half of perpetrators and victims of sexual assault were drunk at the time...alcohol accounted for 2,000 bed nights every day in hospitals and three out of 10 emergency attendances."

Suicide has been closely connected to alcohol throughout the world. Depression is frequently a result of heavy drinking and in turn leads to such hopelessness that suicide is seen as the only way out. It is also the influence of alcohol that grants the 'fool's courage' needed to take that final terrible step which normally would be feared.

Between 2003 and 2005, in Ireland, almost one third (31%) of all car crash deaths were alcohol-related. Where Blood Alcohol Concentration levels were available for drivers killed, almost six out of ten had alcohol in their blood.

Between 1992 and 2002, in Ireland, there was a 400% increase in reports of drunkenness, and between 2003 and 2007, alcohol-related offences increased by 30%. This is not a problem that is going away but is very much on the increase especially amongst the young. We are sowing the wind in our nations and will reap a tornado unless the Lord sends a gracious national revival in each western nation.

Statistics in America for alcohol related car crashes are beyond belief. At least 40% of all car crash fatalities are alcohol related. Someone is killed every 45 minutes, and injured every two minutes by someone under the influence of alcohol. This is America's leading known criminal cause of death each year.

Whilst writing this book I have listened to and read report after report from the medical and political professions in Ireland warning of the serious damage that alcohol is doing to the nation. These reports are constantly broadcast by the secular media in a consistent and serious manner.

Each time I drive into my local city of Limerick, I pass a large flashing sign which states, "Never drink and drive." In Northern Ireland a regularly repeated television advert warns that, "Every drink increases your risk of crashing."

It is no surprise that in January 2013, a proposal was made in South Africa, to change and reduce the legal drink-driving limit to **zero** toleration. In other words, even the most modest amounts of alcohol in the blood would no longer be acceptable for those who are going to drive on the roads. In a country where death by road accidents is astronomic, the realization has come that abstinence is the only answer—not moderation.

In 2008 and 2009, British news media and national newspapers broadcast the terrible crisis of alcohol abuse amongst the nation's teenage females. In just five years between 2003 and 2008, the number of young teen females aged between 14 and 17 years old, who were treated for alcohol poisoning, increased by 90%.

Britain is now notorious as one of the top runners in Europe for teen alcohol abuse through weekend binging. National statistics are twice as bad in Britain as in the United States. This problem so dramatically increased in the first decade of the new millennium that the eyes of the whole nation were fixed upon it.

In one survey in Britain it was revealed that one in ten young females had sex while intoxicated, which they later regretted. The same percentage did so without any form of contraception. The high rate of teen pregnancy is closely associated and intrinsically connected with this national drink problem.

During the 1990s, when drug abuse was at its height, it was estimated that **alcohol killed twenty times more** teenagers than did heroin or ecstasy amounting to two million deaths annually worldwide. Professors, doctors and politicians believe this is but the tip of the iceberg. It is being called not only a national epidemic but **an international epidemic**. A whole generation of young people are playing Russian roulette with their health and life.

In Britain, a 15 year old girl is far more likely to get drunk than a 15 year old boy. These young ladies will be the major moulding influence upon the next generation. The morality of a nation is gauged and standardized by mothers. As mothers go, so goes the nation.

Even 10% of eight year olds are now recorded as indulging in this national pastime. This should not be surprising when we consider that single mothers and parents are setting the example which these young ones are following.

Twice as many marriages end in divorce due to the affects of alcohol as adultery. Often drinking results in physical abuse or inexcusable neglect of home, bills and children. This leads to court cases, heartache and a further moral collapse of society.

The number of people being admitted to British hospitals as a result of drinking too much alcohol has more than doubled. According to medical stats two out of three of all those who die by drowning or choking are due to alcohol. In Ireland, 25% of all visits to A&E (emergency) are drink related.

During my late teens, I knew of numbers of cases of those who almost died from choking when lying in a drunken state, but who were mercifully saved by someone at the scene who was trained in first aid.

In the UK 25% of all accidents in the workplace involve intoxicated workers. Drinkers also take four times as many days off work as abstainers. Recent research across a number of nations reveals that it is the **light and moderate drinkers who cause 87% of all problems in the work place.** There is not one realm of society where alcohol is not spreading its deadly, damaging and deceptive influence.

We could easily go through the statistics of all western nations and find a similar strong connection between crime and the consumption of alcohol not to mention a great host of social ills. We are but lightly skimming over the tragic level of crime and social problems produced in each nation as a result of drinking alcohol.

In our law courts and in our legal system those who commit criminal acts under the influence of alcohol are often treated more sympathetically because they act out of character under its influence or have no memory of the criminal act.

However, in reality an individual should take this into consideration at the first drink and be held fully responsible for the decision to drink a substance which can lead them to criminal acts. The guilt of crime starts with the first drink.

It seems that various secular government departments and national newspapers have a greater concern over these facts than local churches and their leaders. Doctor's look on horrified, politicians put out statements of their utter shock, and the police constantly give forth strong warnings.

When is the church going to wake up? When are local pastors going to start lifting up their voices? Where is the concern of Christian parents? Where are the prophets in the church who will awaken the slumbering conscience of the church? Where are the tears of brokenness and the fervent prayers for this lost world?

Spiritual
Not only is alcohol dangerous to the body and soul but also to the eternal destiny of every individual. Alcoholic wine is portrayed time and time again in the Bible to be as dangerous as a serpent's bite which kills. *"Their wine is the poison of dragons, and the cruel venom of asps"* (Deut.32:33). The ancients drew on the most poisonous of animals in order to convey the thought of fermented wine being poisonous.

The word used here for poison is, *chemah*, which is also used in Hosea 7:5, *"In the day of our king the princes have made him sick with bottles of wine; he stretched out his hand with scorners."* The same word for poison is here translated as bottles. It can read "made him sick with poison of wine." In Hosea's day the princes made the king sick with this poisonous alcoholic wine. As a result he stretched forth his hand to drink with scorners. Alcohol poisons morality and spirituality.

Solomon instructs us in Proverbs 23:31-32, *"Look not thou upon the wine **when** it is red, when it giveth his colour in the cup, when it moveth itself aright. At the last it biteth like a serpent, and stingeth like an adder."*

This scripture reveals that there is a certain time *"**when**"* wine cannot be looked upon or drunk. There is a time when wine is compared to a poison drink. There is a time when wine is as deadly as a serpent. There is a time when it is not even safe to look upon wine.

"Look not thou upon the wine when..." (23:31). He does not just say *"look not thou upon wine."* He inserts the important word **when** clearly implying that there is a time *when* it is safe to look upon it and a time *when* it is not safe to look upon it.

The context reveals that it is **when wine is fermented** that it is not safe to look upon it. This drink which is called *wine* is either safe or dangerous depending on its form or nature. It is called *wine* when it is unfermented and still called *wine* after it is fermented.

What does this scripture mean by *"wine when it is red"*? This is explained by Rod Phillips, in, *A Short History of Wine*, when he describes ancient wine production.

He says, "Actual grape juice is always light-coloured, no matter what the colour of the skin or flesh of the grape, and red wine is given its colour in the fermentation process, when the red or black grape skins remain in the fermentation process, in contact with the juice. It is the duration of this contact that largely determines the colour of the finished wine."[7]

Fermented wine in ancient times was associated with being red or dark so when Scripture instructs us to not look upon it when it is red, it is pointing out just one, but certainly not the only mark, given as a warning sign that the drink may contain alcohol.

Please note that he says: *"when it giveth his colour in the cup."* This is a test applied when actually in the cup; held in the hand. The word "colour" literally means its fountain, countenance or character. When in the cup you can test it and allow it to reveal its character.

Again this is proved by the statement: *"when it moveth itself aright."* I'm sure we have all seen wine tasters swirl the wine in a glass then hold it up to look at it in the light. What are they looking for? After they 'swirl' the wine, it runs down the inside surface of the glass to form what is called *legs*. *Legs* are used to discern the **alcoholic content** of the wine. The slower it moves down or *walks down* the glass the higher the alcoholic content.

In this passage in Proverbs the term *"moveth itself"* is the Hebrew word *halak* meaning to 'walk.' The word *"aright"* means in a straight or upright manner. So this was indeed a very ancient practice in discerning the alcoholic content. This phenomenon reveals the presence of alcohol within wine and stands as a warning.

In the light of all this, verse 31 commands, *"Look not thou upon the wine when it is red, when it giveth his colour in the cup, when it moveth itself aright."* This is saying: **do not look upon it when it is fermented and when you can discern that it has an alcoholic content.**

So in these verses we see that there are two different types of wine: one which is safe to drink and another which must not even be looked upon. This is not a description of

---

[7] p.40, *A Short History of Wine*, Rod Philips

unfermented wine; it is a clear description of alcoholic wine. Here is a command to not even look upon such a drink.

The writer knows that the drink itself is dangerous—not just its abuse. He also knows that this problem is not dealt with by advising moderation in drinking. He places a ban upon the first look which leads to the first drink. The word used here for *"look"* means 'to fix your eyes upon it, to gaze at it, to consider or take heed to it'. This is not talking about a mere look at it, but a real lust for it, with the intention of drinking it in order to experience an effect that only alcohol produces.

We know that Jesus taught that if a man were to look upon a woman to lust after her, it was equivalent to committing adultery. In this Proverb the writer is dealing with the root and the heart of the problem of drunkenness. His instruction is, don't even look upon such a drink with a desire to drink it, because the end of such a desire is disastrous for a great many. Such a look at alcoholic wine could be equivalent in sinfulness to the actual act of drunkenness.

When Lot and family were rescued from the destruction of Sodom and Gomorrah the angel commanded, *"Escape for thy life; look not behind thee, neither stay thou in all the plain"* (Gen.19:17, 26). But Mrs. Lot decided to take just one look and as a result she was turned into a pillar of salt. She did not take the command literally. She must have thought 'just one look.' **Many in this hour are not taking the written Scriptures literally.**

Let's look closer at the description of this wine in Proverbs 23. It says *"at the last it biteth."* In other words it does not initially reveal its danger. At first it may seem fun and innocent but in the end it will bite like a serpent.

Fermented wine is warned against in the strongest possible terms in these scriptures by likening it to the bite of a serpent. Drinking alcoholic wine is like drinking poison. It is deadly. The only way to treat a drink that has such inbred dangers is to not even look at it.

Leaders in every age of the church have warned of the poison of fermented wine. Jerome (346-420) who translated the Bible into Latin and who lived in Rome for several years, and outside Bethlehem in Israel for over thirty years, abstained from and warned against the use of all strong drink and fermented wine:

"If experience gives me a right to advise...I would begin by urging you and warning you, as Christ's spouse, to avoid wine as you would a poison. For wine is the final weapon used by demons against the young."[8]

John Wesley (1703-1791) wrote: "You see the wine when it sparkles in the cup, and are going to drink of it. I tell you there is poison in it! and, therefore, beg you to throw it away. You answer, 'The wine is harmless in itself.' I reply, Perhaps it is so; but still if it be mixed with what is not harmless, no one in his senses, if he knows it at least, unless he could separate the good from the bad, will once think of drinking it. If you add, 'It is not poison to me, though it be to others'; then I say, Throw it away for thy brother's sake, lest thou embolden him to drink also. Why should thy strength occasion thy weak brother to perish, for who Christ died?"[9]

Contemporary doctors and scientists still constantly call the alcohol contained in various fermented wines and various other strong drink a poison and a drug. It is no surprise then that international magazines, national newspapers, secular books on alcohol and a host of other sources all say the very same thing. The secular world certainly supports the clear statement of Scripture.

This poisonous drink spoken of in Proverbs 23 has frequently been the doorway to all manner of sin and has often carried a man where he thought he would never go. In verse 33, it says, *"Thine eyes shall behold strange women, and thine heart shall utter perverse things."* A man who would not normally do this would do it when under the influence of alcohol. Alcohol leads to moral and spiritual break down and will end finally in destruction without remedy.

In verses 29-30 we read of other dire consequences for an individual under the influence of alcoholic wine: *"Who hath woe? Who hath sorrow? Who hath contentions? Who hath babbling? Who hath wounds without cause? Who hath redness*

---

[8] p.25, vol.6, *Letters of the post Nicene Fathers*
[9] Sermon 140, *On Public Diversions*, John Wesley

of eyes? They that tarry long at the wine; they that go to seek mixed wine."

It is in the light of all this that the Bible warns in Proverbs 20:1 *"Wine is a mocker, strong drink is raging: and whosoever is deceived thereby is not wise."*

And again it warns about close association with those who are given over to drinking alcohol or to a glutton's lifestyle: *"Be not among winebibbers; among riotous eaters of flesh: For the drunkard and the glutton shall come to poverty: and drowsiness shall clothe a man with rags"* (Prov.23:20-21). (Note: those who over-eat are put in the same bracket as drunkards.)

The sum total of the evidence set forth in this chapter is that **alcohol destroys internally, externally and eternally.** How can any Christian continue to drink socially in a manner they call moderation when they hear all of these facts?

If the Church is not alarmed at the facts, how do we ever expect the world to be woken up from its drunken party which is taking it rapidly to an eternal Hell? Multitudes are pouring into Hell aided and speeded on their way by alcohol. They leave this life in a happy stupor only to wake in the next utterly sober realising it is fearfully and eternally too late!

While Satan uses this deadly poison to destroy millions and to aid his work in sending nations to Hell, the Church raises her voice and puts forth her efforts to defend her right and liberty to socially drink alcohol.

CHAPTER 4
STRONG DRINK

Time after time, a distinction is drawn in the Old Testament between, *"wine"* and *"strong drink."* What is the difference? Let's first define what *"strong drink"* is. In the Hebrew it is the word *shekar,* which is taken from the root word *shakar* meaning 'to drink abundantly or drink until you're full'. When an intoxicating drink is drunk, the consequences are obvious.

Throughout the whole Old Testament the drinking of *"strong drink"* is condemned outright. Only in one single reference is it spoken of in any positive light, and that is in relation to religious offerings at festivals (Deut.14:26). At this festival the *shekar* was not drunk, but poured out as a drink offering before the Lord (Num.28:7). From this it would seem clear that *shekar* always defines an alcoholic drink.

It is mentioned 23 times out of which 21 times it is translated as *"strong drink"*, once as *"strong wine"*, and once as *"drunkards."* In 20 of these mentions, *wine* (*yayin*) is mentioned in tandem with it and usually appears before it. The connecting factor between these two is that they are condemned for their influence upon mankind.

It would seem from this that when *yayin* is mentioned in connection with *shekar* it is specifically narrowing this generic term to the specific meaning of alcoholic wine. Any form of

43

drink that has the ability to intoxicate because of its alcoholic character is clearly condemned in Scripture.

Although *"strong drink"* is distinct in the Bible from alcoholic *"wine"*, in its chemical makeup it is closely aligned and associated with wine because of its intoxicating influence. The common denominator is **ethyl** alcohol.

The reason why wine and strong drink are distinguished from each other is that wine of course comes from the vine and is squeezed from grapes, whereas strong drink can be taken from grain, barely, honey, dates, pomegranates or other such fruits and sources. It would seem that *shekar* is any alcoholic drink not taken from grapes which has the ability to intoxicate. This means that *shekar* is a generic term for all intoxicating drinks *excluding* wine.

Nowhere is there any instruction to be moderate, careful or temperate in using *shekar,* and neither is there any instruction to be moderate in drinking any alcoholic drink. There is not one single instance where it is called a blessing to God's people, or called a gift from God. Any drink whose character and nature is that of intoxication is condemned.

We are told in Proverbs 20:1, *"Wine is a mocker, strong drink is raging: and whosoever is deceived thereby is not wise."* The use of that little word, *"is"*, in this scripture shows us that this is the character of these drinks. Wine, *"is a mocker."* Strong drink *"is raging."* It is very obvious that this is not the character of a simple fruit drink but of an alcoholic drink.

The word *"raging"* means to make a loud noise, uproar or a great commotion. This is the character of any fruit drink which is fermented, and this is the result produced by it. We are also told that anyone misled or led astray by this deceptive drink, into actions which cause them to make mistakes or to transgress God's Word, are not *"wise."*

Almost every time that *shekar* is mentioned it is in the context of abstaining from it. It was not drunk by those in the wilderness in order that they might know the Lord (Deut.29:6); the priests were forbidden to drink it (Lev.10:9), as were the Nazarites (Num.6:3); Manoah's wife and his son Samson were told to abstain from it (Jdg.13:4, 7, 14); Hannah chose to abstain from it (I Sam.1:15), and kings and princes are clearly commanded to abstain from it at all times (Prov.31:4). It is called a mocker (Prov.20:1). Drunkards who were drinkers of strong drink sang mocking songs about David and his piety (Ps.69:12); those who ran after it were condemned (Isa.5:11), as were those who had strength to mingle it (5:22). Those who drunk it were warned that they would experience bitterness (24:9); priests and prophets were 'out of the way' through drinking it (28:7), and others staggered as a result of drinking it (29:9). Those who filled themselves with it were dulled to reality and future consequences (56:12) and those who promoted it in their prophecies were exposed as walking in falsehood and lies (Mich.2:11).

In the light of this can we honestly think that the Bible encourages a man to drink intoxicating drinks?

Is there one verse to encourage us to drink strong drink? Yes, actually there is: Proverbs 31:6, *"Give strong drink unto him that is ready to perish, and wine unto those that be of heavy hearts."*

This verse is in the very same chapter where kings and princes are strictly forbidden to drink it (31:4-5). It is placed here in contrast with the virtue of abstinence. This command to kings and princes does not mean that others may partake of fermented wine and strong drink.

In this one singular verse, we are told that if strong drink is going to be used then let it be given to a man that is ready to perish. This is a unique and very extreme case. It is only under these circumstances that a man should be given such a drink. This verse is not commending or encouraging this practice but pointing out an extreme occasion when strong drink was used.

It is well known that in ancient days if a criminal was to suffer a lingering, horrible painful death he was given such a drink to numb his senses. This is the only possible biblical example where fermented wine and strong drink could be used with any sort of reasonable explanation.

Apart from a man *"ready to perish"* or of a *"heavy heart"*, no one has the right to justify the drinking of alcohol. These cases show utter helplessness and hopelessness. The reason that such a man drinks alcohol is to *"forget his poverty, and remember his misery no more."* Some would have us believe that the best the Spirit of God can do is to counsel a man in trouble to hide himself in a bottle of wine or in a glass of strong drink until his mind is so numbed that he forgets his trouble.

It is amazing that pro-drinkers have used this very verse as a text to prove that strong drink is allowable and even commanded or commended. If this is the best verse they can come up with then we know that they are pretty desperate in trying to prove that alcohol is allowed by God. There is no teaching in these verses concerning the moderate consumption of alcohol.

"Strong drink" (*sikera*) is used only once in the New Testament when the angel of the Lord appears to Zacharias in order to inform him of the birth of his son, John the Baptist. He gives him the clear instruction that the child *"shall drink neither wine nor strong drink* [**sikera**]*"* (Lk.1:15).

When we read the word *"strong"* we of course think of the contemporary strong drinks of our own day which frequently contain as much as 40% alcohol. But the word *"strong"* in *"strong drink"* does not appear in the original Hebrew and is not translated directly from *shekar*. Neither is it the same as contemporary strong drinks.

The *shekar* of Bible days normally contained no more than 14% alcohol, remembering that only with hard work can wine producers produce a 14% alcoholic content but more normally the end result is 10-12%.

Many of today's alcoholic drinks have a far greater alcoholic content than anything imagined or mentioned in the ancient world. Fortified wines contain 15-20%, Sherry 18-20%, Port wine 20%, liquor and spirits 40%, Whiskey and Rum 60%. The world's most expensive and strongest beer, which is more potent than Whiskey or Brandy, and 16 times more potent than a standard Lager, was released in Scotland in 2012. It is very aptly called *Armageddon* and has a mind-blowing alcohol content of 65%.

There can be no doubt that all contemporary drinks containing these sky-high percentages of alcohol are utterly condemned by God's Word.

Without a shadow of doubt, these drinks and substances which affect the human brain and body by dulling it, numbing it, undermining its clarity, perverting it, changing or altering it, are all condemned even if they are not explicitly named in the Bible. This includes narcotic drugs too, such as cannabis (hash), *Ecstasy*, and a host of other mind-altering drugs not named but certainly covered by the clear teaching and principles of Scripture. Just as many justify the moderate use of alcohol, so some are now trying to justify the moderate use of drugs like cannabis and no doubt this will become more common in the future. It would be hypocritical for those who justify the use of alcohol to then condemn the use of mind-altering drugs. Of course those who stay with the written Scriptures will reject all of these brain-numbing substances.

The well-known Scottish drink, Whiskey, derived its name from the Gaelic word *usquebaugh* meaning *water of life*, but this drink is a long way from being a water of life. It is in fact a water of death—poison in the truest sense. No wonder that such drinks have been called the *Devils Vomit*. It is remarkable that men would put such drinks into their systems but more remarkable that Christians would follow their example and try to justify it by the Bible.

At the lowest end of the scale we find Lager at 4-5%, Beer at 3-10%, and Stout at 5-10%. Because of these lower percentages, some Christians try to justify that these drinks are not nearly as strong as biblical wines. But the fact remains that **it is alcohol itself that is so strongly condemned in the Bible not a specific percentage of alcohol.**

When we read of strong drink in the Bible it includes all drinks containing either a higher or lower level of alcohol than is normally found in wine. A low alcoholic drink (light beer) is as much condemned as a spirit with high alcohol content.

In Isaiah 5:22, we read *"Woe unto them that are mighty to drink wine, and men of strength to mingle strong drink:"* The two terms (*yayin* and *shekar*) appear together here, so we know that the wine is intoxicating. Here is a woe or warning against those who have a reputation at being able to handle their drink, or for drinking much.

It is also a woe and warning against those who 'are strong to mingle strong drink': these have great power, ability or skill to mingle strong drink. Strong drink was not sufficient for them. They desired a stronger drink than the common 14% of alcohol, which was considered poison to the wise.

This was the ancient practice of mixing some drug like myrrh or opium with the drink to make it much stronger. Here is a grave warning for those who desire or who go out of their way to produce a stronger drink than normal. If the strong drink of the Bible is condemned, then anything stronger should come with heightened warning.

Solomon sets forth a full list of serious heartaches for those who, *"go to seek mixed wine"* (Prov.23:30). This desire to feel and experience a strong intoxicating influence is strongly warned against and a man who plays with such a desire, habit or recreation is playing with something very dangerous.

This mixing of drinks to make them stronger is set in stark contrast to the practice of mixing unfermented wine with honey, milk or water: *"Wisdom hath...mingled her wine"* (Pro 9:1-2). This wise mixture produced a harmless but tasty drink. This is in contrast with mixing strong drink to make it stronger.

Mohammad, the founder of Islam, in the early years of his religious life, had a problem with his closest associates who indulged in alcohol and who were frequently drunk. This led to him instituting total abstinence from alcohol which has been taught to Muslims throughout the ages, down to the present day (although present-day reality or adherence to this 'law' differs much across the Islamic world). Islam, however, does not forbid hash and other drugs. This is true legalism. They make a law of abstinence from alcohol, but indulge in other substances which create the same brain-numbing effects—and worse. This is utter hypocrisy.

Fruit Juice vs. Alcohol
It is clear to any unprejudiced person that there is a world of difference and a very great distinction between the influence, effects and consequences of drinking grape juice or fruit juice, as opposed to drinking alcohol.

These two drinks are separated by fermentation. Their very nature is distinct and different. **One is natural the other is the product of decay in a fallen world**. One is harmless the other is as dangerous as any substance on earth. One is condemned with good reason; the other is commended with good reason. Any child, pregnant mother or frail person may take fruit juice without concern but the same individuals should stay away from alcohol.

Many dangers are connected to the use of alcohol but these dangers are not at all reckoned to fruit juice. Alcohol at best must be handled with utmost care and consideration, but fruit juice is free from such characteristic dangers.

A lion, before the fall of Adam, would gladly lie down with a lamb and will do so again according to Isaiah (11:6). We see from this that the fall of man changed the nature of the lion from gentleness to ferociousness; from being adored to being feared. The same is true of wine. A fruit drink created by God for the good, nourishment and refreshment of man has now become a corrupt drink that destroys mankind. The dangers inherent in alcohol are not present in fruit juice.

When a genuine believer is faced with a choice between two such different drinks, what is he to choose? What would the Lord have him to choose? If a person is going to drink alcohol but do his best to stop short of coming under its effects, why drink it at all?

Surely the main reason why people drink alcohol either moderately or to its fullest degree is because of its *effect*? If a believer desires to avoid the many dangers connected to drinking alcohol and to take heed to the serious warnings in the Bible concerning it, why walk close to the line by taking it at all?

Why would a genuine believer choose alcohol rather than multiple fruit drinks which are safe, refreshing, enjoyable, tasty and clearly created by God without any danger of undermining physical and mental faculties?

The God of the Bible is not the God of alcohol or of intoxicating influences—no matter what the degree of consumption is. He does not delight in any Christian numbing his brain, his senses, or undermining his moral restraints. The

God of the Bible takes no delight in anyone looking to alcohol for joy and relaxation instead of to God Himself.

Bacchus or Christ?

The first recorded incident of drunkenness from alcohol was Noah. Regrettably it was not the last. *Sumer* was the first civilisation in the new world after the flood which was raised up and populated by Noah's seed. Fermented wine and other intoxicating drinks were not only part of its social life but became an integral part of its religious life.

The religion of ancient Sumer which grew and prospered in the new cities built by Nimrod had little to do with the true religion of *Elohim*—the Creator of Heaven and Earth (Gen.10:8-12). Myth, perversion, rebellion, sin and false religion blossomed and then spread out into all the earth. So also did the practice and custom of drinking fermented drinks. The first great epic still preserved to us concerns Gilgamesh, ruler of Uruk, (Erek in Gen.10:10), who was renowned as a famous drinker and womanizer.

In these first city states, one element which dominated the man-made religion initiated by Nimrod was the Sumerian *gods of intoxication*. (Vines were successfully grown on specially nurtured vineyards on top of the well-known Ziggurats of this era.)

First came Geshtinanna (Mother Vine Stock), followed by Pa-Gestin-Dug and his wife Ninkasi (Lady of the Intoxicating Fruit). Although beer drinking dominated Sumer it was the vine and wine which gave it her initial dominating *gods of intoxication*. Others followed. The state of inebriation was seen as a gift from these gods and a thing to be embraced and enjoyed.

The female priestesses of this pagan religion which spread across Mesopotamia were not allowed to enter a wine shop, to trade in or drink wine or any other intoxicating beverage outside of the temple. If they partook of it outside the temple they could be killed. Wine was a vital part of religious service and its influence on the minds and bodies of these young ladies was reserved for religious worship and religious buildings alone.

After God's judgement at the tower of Babel and the diversifying of the tongues of man into various family units—maybe as many as seventy different tongues—the worship of the wine-god continued but under different names. The worship of the god of wine spread out in every direction to Egypt, Anatolia (Turkey), India, Phoenicia (Lebanon) and Crete (the Minoan kingdom). The name diversified but the god was the same in character, nature and habit.

In Egypt he became known as Osiris, but he became most famous as Dionysus amongst the Minoans, the Mycenaean's and the Greeks (1500–500 BC). The ancient legends, although diverse, state that he was a new-comer and foreigner to Greece who began his journey in Anatolia (Turkey), moved to Mesopotamia and then on into Persia reaching to the eastern cities of Bactria (now part of Afghanistan). He journeyed through Egypt and Syria to make known his religion of social-drinking and intoxication before finally reaching mainland Greece, bringing with him the vine. This was a journey of some 2000 years.

Dionysus, in the days of his youth, is portrayed as a young man with a beautiful feminine face and is strongly connected to homosexuality. He is frequently seen riding upon a panther or lion, or upon a griffin or tiger-led chariot. He is normally either naked or dressed in an animal skin. In later life he is portrayed as an old, bearded, drunk, naked man.

He is the god of wine, singing, dancing, hilarity, games, fancy dress, music, lust and immorality. He was the driving force behind the Greek theatre, pleasure and festivity. Fermented wine was a gift from his hand for the pleasure and enjoyment of mankind.

Accompanying him were young wild dancing females called the Maenad (Bacchae), who led the way in dance, music and general entertainment in the worship of Dionysus. Their name literally means "raving ones" because of their frenzied dance under the influence of wine.

Frequently accompanying the wine-god, Dionysus, was Silenus, who was the oldest, wisest and most drunken of his followers. He is usually depicted on a donkey or with donkey's ears. When intoxicated, Silenus was said to possess special knowledge and the power of prophecy. The special companions of Silenus, were a group of young men called, Satyrs, who had goatish features.

The name Dionysus was changed to Bacchus, when it reached Rome. Throughout his long journey he is increasingly revealed as the one who brought uninhibited freedom, liberty from restraints; removal of self-conscious fear and release from all care and worry. He granted freedom to say and do what would otherwise not be even thought of when not in his presence.

All of these Grecian and Roman fables, gods and customs were well known but strongly and sternly rejected by the early Church raised up under the ministry of the Apostles. Only as it compromised did such things begin to penetrate into the custom of the Church at Rome. Enjoyment of social drinking as 'a gift from God' slowly became Church custom. The necessity of using fermented wine at communion became a law. Rather than warning against intoxication, it was now embraced and became a notable mark of the Catholic Church. Many of her Popes were notorious for their drunken orgies. Through her influence these practices spread throughout many nations as she grew in power, wealth, dominance and influence.

There is good reason for giving the details of some of these pagan characters and customs above, especially those connected with Dionysus and Bacchus, because such pagan customs and gods have even made blatant inroads into the contemporary church of our own day.

C.S. Lewis, who is so well known, so widely read and admired as a brilliant thinker and author, introduces us to the 'god of wine' in his *Narnia* series. In *The Lion, the Witch, and the Wardrobe,* and then more fully in *Prince Caspian,* we are introduced to these pagan gods. In Chapter eleven of the latter book, we see the children in the story accompanied by Aslan and joined by the very characters and creatures we have mentioned who lead the whole gathering in a merry dance to awaken the spirits of the trees and rivers:

"The crowd and the dance round Aslan (for it had become a dance once more) grew so thick and rapid that Lucy was confused...One was a youth, dressed only in a fawn-skin, with vine-leaves wreathed in his curly hair. His face would have been almost too pretty for a boy's, if it had not looked so extremely wild. You felt, as Edmund said when he saw him a few days later, 'There's a chap who might do anything—absolutely anything.' He seemed to have a great many names— Bromios, Bassareus, and the Ram, were three of them. There were a lot of girls with him, as wild as he. There was even, unexpectedly, someone on a donkey."

The party continues all night until they all fall on the ground as the sun rises. Just then Lucy says to Susan: "I know who they are...The boy with the wild face is Bacchus and the old one on the donkey is Silenus...I wouldn't have felt very safe with Bacchus and all his wild girls if we'd met them without Aslan." Then at the end of the dance everyone sits around drinking great amounts of wine from wooden cups and bowls. We all know what would happen if children sat around drinking large amounts of fermented wine. (Note: Lewis did believe and teach that all wine in the Bible was fermented.)

Just think: here are the foremost gods of intoxication from pagan history, leading Aslan, who is supposed to represent Christ, in wild all-night dances. Lewis is introducing these gods with their customs under a Christianized banner. Christian children have been reading this for generations and have been subtly told that the ancient pagan practices connected to wine and strong drink have been made acceptable when endorsed by Christ.

C.S. Lewis, denied many fundamental evangelical doctrines, smoked, drank, wrote books in bars and strongly promoted social drinking. He was no friend of those who abstained and greatly resented preachers who dealt with outward action and conduct.

I'm afraid Mr. Lewis was out of step with the written Scriptures, but strongly influenced by the ideas, ideologies and habits of Bacchus. Hidden beneath the veneer of this 'Christian

Classic' and presented by the wise, sophisticated, intelligent and profoundly balanced pen of Lewis, is the practice of social drinking, supported by the fable of the one-wine theory, promoted through a so-called balanced moderation doctrine, under which we find the names, characters and practice of pagan gods.

Lewis, is but one of many modern liberal scholars and theologians who have drawn a close association, identification and connection between the various pagan wine gods, especially Dionysus and Bacchus, and the person of Jesus Christ.

A liberal scholar, Randall Heskett, published a book called, *Divine Vintage,* at the end of 2012 which taught that these pagan gods and customs of the ancient world were adopted by Israel, who then transformed Jehovah into a wine god and later passed this heritage on to the early Church when Christ was revealed as a new wine god at Cana of Galilee.

Not surprisingly, liberal theologians, past and present, are becoming one of the main moulding influences behind the social-drinking doctrine in Evangelical circles today in promoting a Jesus who approves of alcohol; who claims it as a gift from His own hand; who promotes it as a blessing to His Church and who delights in saints becoming happy and intoxicated through it.

But when Paul deals with such issues in the Church at Corinth during the First Century, he states that these pagan idols and false gods were not gods at all, but demons (*daimonion*), and he goes on to state: *"I would not that ye should have fellowship with devils"* (I Cor.10:18-20). To have *"fellowship"* (*koinonos*) with them means to share, associate, be a companion, a partaker, or partner with them. It means to have things or practices in common with them.

He then goes further in explaining this: *"Ye cannot drink the cup of the Lord, and the cup of devils: ye cannot be partakers of the Lord's Table and of the table of devils"* (verse 21). These gods who are demons have their cup, table and customs, and the church is to have nothing to do with it. These gods, who were actually demons, included Dionysus and Bacchus and we certainly know that their cup was fermented wine and every other intoxicating drink.

Paul states that these are the very demon-gods to which *"Gentiles sacrifice"*. So no Christian at Corinth or in the Church of our day was to fall into line with the customs, habits and doctrines connected with these demons and neither was any Christian to partake of their cup.

Paul is quoting from the book of Deuteronomy 32:17-18 *"They sacrificed unto devils, not to God; to gods whom they knew not, to new gods that came newly up, whom your fathers feared not. Of the Rock that begat thee thou art unmindful, and hast forgotten God that formed thee"*.

The Lord is referred to as Israel's Rock six times in this chapter. This was a song given by Moses to remind them how they forsook the true God, the true Rock, when in the wilderness. In the early stage of the wilderness journey, Israel became idolatrous in serving idols, which were actually demons.

They had gained the knowledge of this idolatry and of the customs of these pagan gods in Egypt. It was these practices which manifested suddenly in the camp of Israel mixing it with the true worship of the true Rock of Israel. By this they stirred the Lord to great jealousy.

In verse 31, Moses calls this god of a confused mixture, *"their rock."* The god they were worshipping, although given the very same name by these rebels as the true God, was actually a counterfeit and imitation of the true Rock. *"For their rock is not as our Rock, even our enemies themselves being judges."* Even the heathen could tell the difference while Israel was deceived. These two rocks were not the same.

In the very next verses the cup and drink of this *foreign rock*, inspired by demons is identified: *"For their vine is of the vine of Sodom, and of the fields of Gomorrah: their grapes are grapes of gall, their clusters are bitter: Their wine is the poison of dragons, and the cruel venom of asps"* (32-33). The drink of these demon gods was fermented wine.

But now contrast this description with faithful Israel at the beginning of this chapter when the Lord kept her, *"as the apple of his eye";* when *"there was no strange god with him."* We see His doctrine falling upon her just as refreshing rain falls upon the herb and grass of the field. We see her separated out from the pagan nations with their various strange gods, but Israel preserved in carrying the true worship of the true Rock (32:1-12).

Please note the drink which she enjoyed in the days when she was free from other gods: *"and thou didst drink the pure blood of the grape"* (v14). This was the freshly pressed unfermented juice of the grape. It was harmless, refreshing, God-given and a blessing. What a contrast to the intoxicating wine brought into the camp of Israel through demonically-inspired gods.

Earlier in this chapter Paul says that Christ was the Rock of Israel in the wilderness but some among the people were overthrown when they lusted for evil things. In verse 10 he says: *"Neither be ye idolaters, as were some of them; as it is written, The people sat down to eat and drink, and rose up to play."* This is quoted directly from Exodus 32:6, in reference to Israel when they sacrificed the gold of their women and children to make the golden calf and then called this false god by the name of the true God (v8).

They then proclaimed *"a feast to the LORD"* (v5-6), at which they ate and drank. This feast was marked by rising up to play (v6), dancing (v19), and nakedness (v25). To *"play"* means 'to laugh outright in merriment or scorn'. This sounds like an intoxicated party and carries all the marks and results of such. It is hard to believe that Israel so quickly forgot her Rock and turned from the *"pure blood of the grape"* to the *"poison of dragons, and the cruel venom of asps."*

So with this backdrop Paul contrasts the cup of blessing which represents the Blood of Jesus Christ, which is given at the communion table, with the cup of devils presented at their tables. The drink at all pagan feasts, acts of worship at their tables and altars was strong drink and fermented wine. In total contrast then, the contents of the cup given by Christ to the Disciples which Paul mentions in the following chapter is always called by Christ the *"fruit of the vine"* (Mt.26:27-29; Mk.14:23-25; Lk.22:17-18; I Cor.11:25-28).

CHAPTER 5
DRUNKENNESS

Foundational to our whole discussion on alcohol is the fact that the teaching of Scripture is so very clear in calling all drunkenness, sin. Every time it is mentioned in Scripture it is condemned in the strongest terms possible and carries pointed warnings concerning eternal judgement.

Sadly, in certain groups which call themselves 'Christian' in our generation, drunkenness is accepted, tolerated, promoted, enjoyed or seen as a mere weakness or sickness. All such excuses for drunkenness are clearly challenged and condemned by the written Word of God. Men and denominations can argue over such things, but God's Word alone has the final say in such matters. Let's look at what the Bible says about drunkenness.

When it comes to descriptions of drunkenness the Bible is unsurpassed. It gives us such clear and well defined descriptions of it, as well as its symptoms and the result of its effects that we could not possibly be in any doubt as to what is being said.

Poverty, drowsiness, woe, sorrow, contentions, babbling, wounds, redness of eyes, addiction, sexual lust and immorality, speaking perverse things in your heart, delusion, passing out into unconsciousness (Prov.23:20-35), violence (4:17), mocking and raging (20:1), forgetfulness, mistakes (31:5), pride, fading beauty, overcome, trodden under foot, erring in vision, out of the way, stumbling in judgement, vomiting, filthiness, untidiness (Isa.28:1, 3, 7-8), reeling to and fro, falling (24:20), sickness, scorn (Hos.7:5), nakedness (Gen.9:21; Lam.4:21), madness (Jer.51.7), transgression, insatiable desire, neglect of home and family, dissatisfaction, self-centredness (Hab.2:5) and much more is connected with drunkenness.

The Bible warns us more than 70 times about the sin of drunkenness and gives us 19 clear examples of intoxication from alcoholic wine. Let's look at just a couple of incidents involving righteous men in the Old Testament who experienced the full effect of drunkenness and the consequences that resulted from it.

Examples of Drunkenness

The first recorded incident of drunkenness in the Bible was that of Noah. He was indeed a righteous man who feared God, but this one-off incident of drunkenness is indeed sad. *"And Noah began to be an husbandman, and he planted a vineyard: And he drank of the wine, and was drunken; and he was uncovered within his tent...And Noah awoke from his wine, and knew what his younger son had done unto him. And he said, Cursed be Canaan"* (Gen.9:20-21, 24-25).

This is the first mention of drunkenness and it stands at the headway of this subject in Scripture as a stark warning to all. This was more than 1,600 years after creation (about 2342 BC) and takes place after the Flood. It takes five to six years to grow the vine to the point of fruit bearing, so it is clear that this act of drunkenness was not immediately after their departure from the Ark on the mountains of Ararat.

Noah's first act upon leaving the Ark was to build an altar of sacrifice in order to worship and pray unto the LORD. Noah was undoubtedly a spiritual man. He had a spotless testimony for 600 years. The Lord considered him perfect in his generation. He walked with God in a covenant relationship of grace and the Lord revealed His secrets to him concerning coming judgement.

It is obvious that Noah had knowledge concerning the cultivation and growth of the vine. This was accomplished at a time when Noah and his family were staying in one place somewhere in the region below Ararat. Producing grapes and then wine must have taken him much consideration, time and care. When he first began to drink of this intoxicating brew, he would have felt the first effects of it which soon led to intoxication. It began with feeling relaxed and happy, and led on to a relief from any concerns. Sadly the alarm bells did not go off or were not heeded by this man of God. In a state of intoxication he either fell into a deep sleep or blanked out.

While in this state of unconsciousness we are told that: *"... [Noah] was uncovered within his tent...And Ham...saw the nakedness of his father..."* Ham's lightness in seeing, then going and telling his brothers is clearly condemned. This act of drunkenness led to great shame and family conflict. But some see even more here.

To 'uncover someone's nakedness' or 'see their nakedness' is at times connected to some form of a sexual act or intercourse (Lev.18:6-19; 20:17-21). Some have thought that this may have been why it says that when he awoke from his stupor, that Noah *"knew what his younger son had done unto him."* The evidence is not clear enough to be dogmatic, but if true, then this was the first homosexual act that we read of in the Bible and it is directly connected to alcohol.

This error of the father gave opportunity for the character of the sons to be revealed. Shem and Japheth acted with purity, honour, devotion, respect and with strong moral convictions. On the other hand the character of Ham is revealed; he acted with mockery, lightness, disrespect and with a carelessness regarding nakedness.

As a result Noah cursed his grandson. Noah did not curse Ham who was guilty but his grandson Canaan. If this curse had fallen upon Ham it would have passed to each of his sons but this curse goes straight to the line of Canaan.

This was a prophecy from the Lord and the Lord knew that Canaan was his father's son. He had inherited the worst of Ham's character and would eventually raise up a wicked people. The Canaanites were later known as some of the most wicked and immoral of ancient peoples.

The second incident of drunkenness was that of Lot. You will remember that he set his tent towards the city of Sodom and Gomorrah, and eventually moved there. He then raised a family in the midst of its gross, abounding iniquity which eventually polluted and destroyed the whole family even though he himself was righteous. This all began with one initial gaze upon ground that looked good to the eye, and which his heart desired (Gen.13:10-13; 14:12; 19:1-38; II Pet.2:7).

After escaping the judgement of God with his two young daughters he took refuge in a cave. Before leaving Sodom they had obviously hurriedly packed some of its intoxicating wine. The daughters, thinking that all mankind had been destroyed, produced a plan to conceive a child by their father by using this alcoholic drink (19:31-36).

It is worth noting that Moses speaks of the *"vine of Sodom"* which grew in the *"fields of Gomorrah"* as that which produces a wine that is considered *"the poison of dragons, and the cruel venom of asps"* (Deut.32:32-33).

In Genesis 19 we are told that these daughters said: *"...let us make our father drink wine, and we will lie with him. And they made their father drink wine that night also..."* This terrible act of incest was the result of drunkenness. These desperate and immoral girls learned their trade in Sodom. They could only fulfil their scheme if he was drunk. This righteous man was led to immorality twice through drinking fermented wine.

He never would have consented if he had had his wits about him. It clearly says that *"he perceived not when she lay down, nor when she arose."* Here was a condition, action, sin and conduct only possible when Lot was under the influence of alcohol. Once under that influence he was not aware of what was happening. In Sodom and Gomorrah he rebuked sinners, but drink removed all conviction, restraint and morals.

Lot was a mature, physically strong man who had much experience, yet could not resist the deadly influence and consequences that are a vital part of alcohol's inbred character. How much less then will young men, women and children escape its deadly effects if not avoided?

Many a young man or woman has played games with alcohol and have been burnt badly by being taken advantage of while under its influence and as a result have lost their virginity. *"Woe unto him that giveth his neighbour drink, that puttest thy bottle to him, and makest him drunken also, that thou mayest look on their nakedness"* (Hab.2:15). It is a medical fact that just a couple of drinks of alcohol raise the testosterone levels released into a woman's bloodstream, which then raises her sex-drive and makes her much more vulnerable than normal to sexual advances. The same amount of drink makes a man willing to take advantage of such a woman.

This world and even some who profess to be Christians will use alcohol to draw others into sin. Those who avoid all such use of alcohol are saved from many dangers.

The environment of the Church is not free of dangers. False converts, tares, goats and wolves will gladly use social drinking for their own advantage and their own ends. Disguised as sheep, they claim pure motives, yet are devils in disguise.

Consequences of Drunkenness

The Greek word for drunkard means: to drink well or fully to the point of saturation of an intoxicating drink; to drink to the point of intoxication. It was the act of drinking beverages made from barley, grapes or pomegranates which were fermented. It was a state in which a man took that which affected and dulled his senses and altered his mode of action, speech, composure and ability.

To be a drunkard was not a one-off act or incident, but **a way of life**. It was not a mere social drink but a practice of drinking alcohol to the point of drunkenness on a habitual basis. It was repeated intoxication—it was a habit of life.

Paul the apostle was very clear when it came to teaching the Church concerning drunkenness: *"Know ye not that the unrighteous shall not inherit the kingdom of God? Be not deceived: neither fornicators, nor idolaters, nor adulterers, nor effeminate, nor abusers of themselves with mankind, Nor thieves, nor covetous, nor drunkards, nor revilers, nor extortioners, shall inherit the kingdom of God"* (I Cor.6:9-10).

Take good note here that Paul teaches the Church at Corinth that a *"drunkard...shall not inherit the kingdom of God."* He will not enter God's kingdom, he is not saved and he is not on his way to Heaven. Paul confirms this again in Galatians 5:21, *"...murders, drunkenness...and such like...they which do such things shall not inherit the kingdom of God."* This could not be clearer.

Again note in the above scripture that Paul says *"...the unrighteous shall not inherit the kingdom of God."* He then goes on to define this unrighteousness by naming several lifestyles including drunkenness. Drunkenness is unrighteousness and will send you to Hell as quickly as murder, idolatry or adultery.

Let us be very clear: unless repented of, drunkenness will send a man to Hell. Sins such as drunkenness were set apart in the Old Testament as so wicked and dangerous to the whole welfare of the community, that God ordained that such a person should be stoned to death.

"And they shall say unto the elders of his city, This our son is stubborn and rebellious, he will not obey our voice; he is a glutton, and a drunkard. And all the men of his city shall stone him with stones, that he die: so shalt thou put evil away from among you; and all Israel shall hear, and fear" (Deut.21:20-21).

In this scripture drunkenness goes hand in hand with rebellion and gluttony. This particular son was not willing to listen to the wise counsel of his parents. He was stubborn. This was no longer a personal family issue. It had now become an issue with which the city elders must deal.

God calls the sin of drunkenness, evil, and says that it must be put away from amongst His people—it cannot be tolerated. While man excuses it, or lightens its seriousness, God condemns it in the strongest possible terms. Much time is spent in scripture defining this sin, revealing how much of a curse it is and how it is to be responded to.

In verse 11, of I Corinthians 6, Paul, goes on to say, *"And such were some of you: but ye are washed, but ye are sanctified, but ye are justified in the name of the Lord Jesus, and by the Spirit of our God."* Those who made up the Corinthian Church had amongst them those who had been drunkards, liars, homosexuals, adulterers and every other manner of sinful lifestyle prior to their salvation.

These converts were now washed, sanctified and justified. They were not only forgiven and washed from their past sin but were changed in character and nature in a manner that made them a new creature in Christ Jesus. They no longer got drunk. They were no longer drunkards.

This is the virtue and power of salvation through the Cross. There is total freedom from the power of alcohol and drunkenness through the Cross. This is not something that must be accepted as a personal weakness. It must be fled from, repented of and forsaken as a part of genuine salvation.

A church that tolerates drunkenness in its midst by those who say that they are Christians are undermining the message of the Cross. They are denying true salvation and destroying the purity of the local church. They are blind to what Christ accomplishes in salvation and are denying sinners the hope of deliverance from their sin of addiction.

'Christian Drunkards'

By using the term 'Christian Drunkard' in no way am I inferring that a man can be a true Christian while at the same time a drunkard. I am however pointing out that Paul deals with the fact that a genuine believer may fall into this destructive sin. In reality this term is an utter contradiction of itself yet such a condition is tolerated in the contemporary Church. A man can die a drunkard but he's put in Heaven by sentimental heretics.

Paul goes much further than just stating that drunkenness is a soul-damning sin. In speaking of those in the Church, who consider themselves Christians and who are called *"brother"* by others, but who begin to regularly get drunk, he says, *"But now I have written unto you not to keep company, if any man that is called a brother be a fornicator, or covetous, or an idolater, or a railer, or a drunkard, or an extortioner; with such an one no not to eat"* (I Cor.5:11).

Paul is very clear. He says that if there is a man in the Church who is considered to be a Christian by others or who calls himself a Christian, yet he gets drunk repeatedly, he is to be dealt with, not ignored, even if he does have a genuine desire to be free. The Church, the Christians who know him or others who come in touch with him, are instructed on how they are to act towards such a so-called *Christian Drunkard*.

First of all they are not to keep *"company"* with him. That means they are not to mix with him or allow him to intermix with them in the fellowship of church gatherings. They must not gather together with him or dwell in unity with him in fellowship as if nothing is wrong. He must be excluded from fellowshipping with them in meetings and in Christian gatherings if he will not forsake his alcohol. He will have to choose between drink and fellowship.

Secondly, they are not even to eat with such a one. So this does not only include church meetings but also social fellowship. In verse thirteen, we are told *"Therefore put away from among yourselves that wicked person."* A so-called Christian who habitually gets drunk is called a *"wicked person."* True Christians who love Jesus and love God's Word must not allow such persons to fellowship amongst them in their meetings or in their homes. Our young people must not see such a lifestyle displayed as acceptable.

This is basic Christian teaching concerning the order and discipline of the local church. Sadly in most churches it is rarely taken seriously. It is all too common for a 'Christian-drunkard' to partake of the Lord's Table each week and to have liberty to fellowship with others without restraint while leaders and other believers say or do nothing.

Please, do take very good note however, that Paul makes it clear in verse 10, that he is not speaking *"of this world"* or people of this world who were outside the Church and outside of Christ because then *"must ye needs go out of the world."* If Christians were commanded not to meet, intermix or eat with drunkards, fornicators, idolaters and such like it would be impossible to live in secular society or be in contact with many family members at all. But Paul is only speaking of those who profess to be Christians and who are expecting to receive an eternal reward.

In verse thirteen, he says, *"them that are without, God judgeth."* And again *"For what have I to do to judge them also that are without?"* So although Paul was clear in his preaching and teaching that drunkards in the world will go to Hell, he makes clear that God will deal with them and judge them, not man or the church. Although sinners are to be warned about the consequence of their sin, the Church cannot discipline them. But while we are not to implement judgement or church discipline upon sinners outside the Church, Paul does say, *"do not ye judge them that are within?"* Of course the answer is, yes: if it becomes evident that those calling themselves Christians in the Church are living in such sin, Christians are to implement church discipline upon them.

It has become increasingly popular to hear Christians say, 'leave it to the Holy Spirit to convict them' or 'leave it to their own conscience' or 'God knows their heart.' But the fact is that we are clearly commanded to be led by the Spirit of God, to obey Scripture in dealing with them over it. To turn a blind eye and to ignore such actions without taking action is disobedience to the revealed will of God.

Recovering a Fallen Brother
Again Paul says in II Thessalonians 3:14-15, *"...have no company with him, that he may be ashamed."* Why is this to be done? This separating from him is with the purpose of making him ashamed of his actions. The purpose of causing him to become *"ashamed"* is that he may come to a realisation of his sin. It is hoped that this act of discipline will cause him to turn his eyes inward, to his inward state, in such a way as to create shame for his actions.

We see in II Thessalonians, 3:14-15, *"...have no company with him, that he may be ashamed. Yet count him not as an enemy, but admonish him as a brother."* Here is a lovely balance. Yes, separate from him, but treat him as a brother and look for him to repent. Seek that he may turn from his sin and return to Christ.

This is not talking of one who has never been delivered from the power of alcohol through a true conversion experience, but rather it is one who shows every sign of having been a true believer and follower of Christ, but has turned to drink or turned back to drink.

All too often, Christians become ashamed of a believer who has fallen into drunkenness. They criticise him harshly and separate from him in such a manner as to count him an enemy rather than a fallen brother. This is wrong. This shows a lack of compassion, concern, and no consciousness of your own frailty. We must treat such a one as a brother and not an enemy.

How do you treat him as a brother rather than an enemy? by admonishing him. To admonish means to call attention to; to warn; to put in mind. It carries the sense of carrying this out with gentleness. If you want to show brotherly love towards such a one you will admonish them. You will point out their sin, you will exhort them to return, you will seek to woo and win them back to Christ.

Separation from identifying with a person's sin does not mean segregation. This act of separation does not mean that you just avoid him. We must preserve a biblical separation from the drunkard who professes to be a Christian, but at the very same time maintain a loving contact with him by which you can bring correction and lead him back to a place of repentance.

"And have no fellowship with the unfruitful works of darkness, but rather reprove them" (Eph.5:11). We are not to settle down in fellowship and communion with those walking in darkness and sin without pointing this out through reproof. Unfruitful works of darkness are those that do not produce the fruit of holiness.

No matter what someone's past testimony may seem to be, if they turn aside from following after the way of the Lord unto drunkenness and die in such a state they will be eternally lost. *"Brethren, if any of you do err from the truth, and one convert him; Let him know, that he which converteth the sinner from the error of his way shall save a soul from death, and shall hide a multitude of sins"* (Jm.5:19-20).

A true Christian may stray, stumble and fall but they prove themselves a true brother in Christ by listening and responding to such admonishing and by returning to Christ. A practising drunkard who calls himself a Christian is called by God, a *"sinner."* Unless he turns he is on a pathway of death. Those who think they can get drunk but go to Heaven are deceived.

Christians must realise that they must labour to turn these so-called Christians as well as sinners from drunkenness, and to know that by doing so they will save souls from Hell. In Leviticus 19:17, we are told that if we see our brother sin but do not rebuke him, it shows that we hate him. And again: *"Open rebuke is better than secret love"* (Prov.27:5). It is a real sign of spirituality for a Christian to labour to restore a fallen brother. *"Brethren, if a man be overtaken in a fault, ye which are spiritual, restore such an one in the spirit of meekness; considering thyself, lest thou also be tempted"* (Gal.6:1).

When I was very young, I heard an old preacher share a principle which has stayed with me over the years. He had made it his principle in dealing with such situations that if after approaching someone who had fallen into serious sin, he saw no change he then took a second person with him who had been successfully recovered from that particular sin. So if the person had fallen into habitual drunkenness he took with him a brother from the Assembly who had been wonderfully restored from such. By this means, hope could be inspired. This second brother who had been successfully recovered would have genuine love and compassion in this situation and faith that Christ can totally restore (Mt.18:15-18; Rom.12:21; Jm.5:19-20).

It is not sufficient to rebuke a fallen brother—we must restore them. That is the goal in view of all godly rebuke. This term *"restore"* means to repair or mend something and is used of the fixing of rent fishing nets. We must labour to restore a fallen brother back to his first estate.

Take good note that we are to do this *"in the spirit of meekness"*, that is in gentleness and humility. Anyone who is going to participate in restoring fallen Christians must have the right heart attitude. This is vital. Pride, arrogance, roughness, mocking and such things will never restore a fallen brother. But more than that, if someone tries to minister to others with such a heart they may well find that they are tempted to fall into sin.

Paul is quick to warn: *"...considering thyself, lest thou also be tempted"* and *"Wherefore let him that thinketh he standeth take heed lest he fall"* (I Cor.10:12). Such ministry should not be approached lightly, casually or proudly, but carefully, prayerfully and humbly.

If and when a brother who has fallen into drunkenness repents with great sorrow over his sin and returns again to Christ, the church ought to embrace him in Christian love. *"...ye ought rather to forgive him, and comfort him, lest perhaps such a one should be swallowed up with overmuch sorrow. Wherefore I beseech you that ye would confirm your love toward him"* (II Cor.2:7-8).

Be careful that such sorrow for his sin or the consequences of his sin does not hinder him in moving on with God. *"...forgive him...comfort him...love him."* Make sure that he is welcomed back with great warmth in a manner that will make him function as a vital part of the body and act in such a manner to aid him from falling into such a lifestyle again.

Such a person who has been restored to a walk of holiness by God's grace can be a wonderful instrument of righteousness to help others also. He is a living testimony that one can be restored and can walk free from the power and influence of alcohol. He is a prodigal son who has returned and been received by his Heavenly Father. A lost sheep, restored to the sheepfold by the Great Shepherd.

CHAPTER 6
LEADERSHIP AND ALCOHOL

Before dealing with social drinking in the Church we must first look at leadership. If this issue is not first dealt with amongst leaders it will not have a wide impact upon the Church. Church leaders have been commissioned by the Lord to lead, guard and feed the sheep. Once they believe correctly, walk correctly and teach correctly on this issue they will become an example which the whole flock may then follow.

In both the Old and New Testaments, qualifications were laid down for those in leadership. When we speak of qualifications we speak of those qualities in a person's life which make them fit, suitable or eligible for leadership.

The great mark of New Testament leadership was not charisma, gifting, ability, ministry or personality but **character**. Only one qualification in Paul's two lists of more than 15 characteristics has anything to do with gifted ability *"apt to teach"*; all the rest have to do with Christian character and conduct (I Tim.3; Tit.1).

More has always been expected of leaders than other believers; leaders are to embody and manifest how all Christians should live as the example for all to see. Most of these qualifications were to be followed and imitated by the whole church. It was the leaders who were to maintain, promote and exemplify the high ideals of what the Lord desired in the whole church.

In these qualifications we see a revealing of the very mind, thought, desire and instruction of God not only for leaders but for all believers. We could say very much about this but we want to concentrate on the issue of alcohol in relation to qualifying or disqualifying leadership.

Old Testament Leadership

In Proverbs 31 we read the words taught to King Lemuel by his Mother. *"It is not for kings, O Lemuel, it is not for kings to drink wine; nor for princes strong drink: Lest they drink, and forget the law, and pervert the judgment of any of the afflicted."* In the previous verse we read that such a thing is *"that which destroyeth kings"* (Prov.31:4-5).

This is an emphatic, 'No', to leaders who would consider taking any alcoholic drink. Twice over in the same verse this wise mother of Israel says *"it is not for kings..."* She is making a clear, strong stand on the issue of taking alcoholic drinks. Today's Church would mock such a wise old mother, yet here Scripture holds her forth with a warning voice to all who have ears to hear.

Please note that there is a very logical reason why Kings should not drink wine or Princes strong drink—it will result in them forgetting God's Word and also will impair their ability to judge issues, which will greatly affect many people who are in trouble.

Alcohol will interfere with the task of a king and his ability to faithfully fulfil his duty. But more than that, abstinence is not restricted to 'active duty' as some try to infer from this text. She does not instruct them to be abstinent on duty—she states emphatically that such a drink is not at all for Kings. No exception. A king and a prince cannot separate themselves from their calling. A king is always a king, and a king should never use intoxicating drinks.

Neither is this a call to moderation in drinking wine and strong drink—it is a clear call to total abstinence. The means by which kings and princes are prevented from abusing alcohol is to not drink it at all, at any time, under any conditions.

This is not a legalistic command but a wise exhortation. Such a thing is known in history for utterly wiping out king and kingdom. Is it any wonder then that the mother of King Lemuel taught him this prophecy by drilling it into him from a young age? The Scriptures give us many warnings of great kings who were killed while celebrating in a drunken stupor or who acted foolishly under the influence of alcohol. King Elah of Israel (I Kgs.16:9), Benhadad, king of Syria (I Kgs.20:16) and Belshazzar the last king of Babylon (Dan.5:1-6) were all killed when drunk. King Ahasuerus of Persia who ruled from India to Ethiopia acted unwisely in relation to his Queen when he was merry from drinking (Est.1:10-12). Many other examples could be related from secular history of great leaders who made foolish mistakes because of the influence of alcohol.

When God was establishing the spiritual ministry of the priesthood in Israel He commanded Aaron saying: *"Do not drink wine nor strong drink, thou, nor thy sons with thee, when ye go into the tabernacle of the congregation, lest ye die: it shall be a statute for ever throughout your generations: And that ye may put difference between holy and unholy, and between unclean and clean; And that ye may teach the children of Israel all the statutes which the LORD hath spoken unto them by the hand of Moses"* (Lev.10:9-11).

This was not just a command to not be drunk but a command to totally and utterly abstain from even one drink of an intoxicating drink. Again the wisdom of God is revealed in this for wine and strong drink will not aid or help this ministry but only hinder an individual in accomplishing it. But more than this, ministry under such an influence is not at all acceptable to God.

The Lord warns that if they approach ministry with any alcoholic influence upon them which impairs or alters their faculties, He will kill them. If you read the context of this chapter you will see that this is exactly what Aaron's two sons, Nadab and Abihu, had done.

In verse one we read: *"And Nadab and Abihu, the sons of Aaron, took either of them his censer, and put fire therein, and put incense thereon, and offered strange fire before the LORD, which he commanded them not."* This foolish act was carried out under the influence of alcohol. We are not told that they were drunk. But they most certainly had been drinking alcohol. It might have been one drink or several, but in either case it was sufficient to be counted as disobedience to God and to be judged.

Although drinking alcohol was condemned for all of God's people only leaders were under immediate threat of death if they disobeyed. This must have caused all the people to reflect deeply on the wrong of drinking fermented wine and to walk in the fear of God.

Isaiah the prophet had to deal with drunkenness in the lives of the priests and prophets of God's people. He said: *"But they also have erred through wine, and through strong drink are out of the way; the priest and the prophet have erred through strong drink, they are swallowed up of wine, they are out of the way through strong drink; they err in vision, they stumble in judgment. For all tables are full of vomit and filthiness, so that there is no place clean"* (Isa.28:7-8).

Here are spiritual leaders who are a vital part of the religious machinery of the nation who have come under the influence of wine and strong drink which causes their prophetic vision to go astray into deception and causes the steadfast clear judgement of the priests to become the moveable, shifting opinion of a compromiser without backbone.

Isaiah speaks in chapter 56 concerning the Shepherds who were called to be Watchmen of God's people. He says they had become blind, ignorant, dumb, greedy, and slothful lacking any understanding. Then in verse twelve, he says, *"Come ye, say they, I will fetch wine, and we will fill ourselves with strong drink; and tomorrow shall be as this day, and much more abundant."*

These Shepherds and Watchmen actively encouraged the drinking of alcohol amongst the people to the point of drunkenness. This had become a part of their message. This revealed just how corrupt the ministry had become in Isaiah's day. These Shepherds thought they could continue in ministry without God judging them.

Who can doubt that leadership which is free from the influence of alcohol is highly commended and encouraged in the

Old Testament but a ministry influenced by alcohol is condemned in the strongest possible terms.
We are only skimming over a few verses here. There are many others, but let's look at the New Testament Church.

New Testament Leadership

The Old Testament requirements of leadership for Kings, Princes and Priests were most certainly not of a higher standard than the eldership in the New Testament Church. In fact there is a continuation of unity and agreement concerning the conduct of leadership in both dispensations and the thought of God concerning it.

Paul lays out very clear qualifications for eldership or leadership in the local church. In his letters to Titus and Timothy he gives two similar lists of characteristics which should be looked to in appointing local leaders. Three of these concern wine or have a connection to wine.

As we deal with wine and leadership in the New Testament we must remember that the word for wine (*oinos*) in the New Testament is a generic term exactly like *yayin* in the Old Testament. Each time we read of wine (*oinos*) in the New Testament we must discern, study and understand if this generic term is referring to wine which is simply the sweet juice of the grape, or if it is wine which has gone through the process of fermentation.

It will be seen as we study Paul's use of *oinos* (wine) in his writings to Timothy and Titus that confusion occurs if it is assumed that each time *oinos* is used it always means a fermented drink. The exact same confusion will occur if we think it always means unfermented grape juice.

As we now approach Paul's, instructions to Timothy, in reference to wine and leaders we must rightly divide the Word of God to understand exactly what he is saying in each text.

You will remember that, Paul, instructs, Timothy: *"Drink no longer water, but use a little wine for thy stomach's sake and thine often infirmities"* (I Tim.5:23). Almost all commentators are agreed that, Paul, is instructing, Timothy, to 'No longer drink water exclusively.' We shall give a full explanation of this scripture in a later chapter, but for now please note that until this point, Timothy totally abstained from drinking fermented wine *as well as* from new wine, which was unfermented.

In life and ministry, Timothy, was known as one who only drank water. Throughout his early ministry, travels and oversight in apostolic ministry alongside Paul it would seem clear that he did not drink wine, either fermented or unfermented.

We will see as we go through the following chapters that fermented wine is strongly condemned in God's Word, whereas unfermented wine is most certainly allowed. Therefore, Paul, is here instructing Timothy, to take unfermented wine for his stomach.

To this same Timothy, Paul gives instruction concerning wine in relation to being led in the choice of the right leaders for local churches. Out of more than 15 qualifications which Paul lists when instructing Timothy and Titus on the choice of local leaders (bishops), three have a direct bearing upon the issue of wine and alcohol in relation to the qualification of elders (I Tim.3; Tit.1). This ought not to be ignored or made light of.

The first of the qualifications associated with wine that Paul instructs Timothy to look out for is *"vigilance"* (3:2). This same instruction is given for deacon's wives (v11) and older men in the church (Tit.2:2). This important word, vigilance or *nephalios* in Greek, is given as a qualification for leadership so we must understand exactly what it means.

Nephalios is taken from *nepho* which means 'to be free from the influence of intoxicating drinks.' The word *nepho,* and the family of words associated with it, were known and used in secular Greek society in the First Century for **total abstinence**—abstaining from alcoholic wine.

Josephus (37-100 AD), writes of the Jewish priests in the First Century: "Those who wear the sacerdotal garments are without spot and eminent for their purity and sobriety (*nephalioi*), not being permitted to drink wine as long as they wear those garments."[10] Josephus used this word three times in

---

[10] Josephus, Antiquities of the Jews 3, 12, 2, trans. William Whiston, *Josephus Complete Works* (Grand Rapids, 1974), p. 81.

his writings with the clear sense of abstaining from drinking wine. That which was expected of the priests during their ministry in the temple is now expected of church leaders as a part of normal daily life, character and conduct.

Speaking of Hannah as a type of a true convert and follower of the Lord, Philo (20 BC-50 AD) says: "...the soul goes on to deny that it drinks wine or strong drink, boasting in its being continually sober *(neephein)* throughout the whole of its life."[11] He also writes of those who, "put the cup of strong drink to their lips" and so, "eliminate soberness *(nephalion)* from their soul."

Clement, of Alexandria (150-215 AD), says, "I therefore admire those who have adopted an austere *(nephalion)* life, and who are fond of water, the medicine of temperance, and flee as far as possible from wine, shunning it as they would the danger of fire."[12]

When Paul, instructs in these scriptures written to Timothy, and Titus, that the elders, deacons wives, and older men were to be *"vigilant"* it was clearly understood in the First Century that he meant they must be known as abstainers from intoxicating wine.

The fact that Paul instructs Timothy to take a little wine for his stomach but here instructs that leaders should be abstainers from wine reveals a distinction in the kind of wine. Fruit of the grape is not only allowed but is commended or at least considered profitable. But fermented wine is never spoken of in such a manner.

Timothy and Titus are instructed to search out and appoint leaders who abstain from wine. They are also instructed to teach the churches that all the mature men and women in the assembly should be known as abstainers. Paul would never contradict himself in the same letter.

But Paul goes further than just calling leaders to total abstinence. In I Timothy 3:2, he writes "*...apt to teach; Not*

---

[11] *On drunkenness,* Philo
[12] *Clement of Alexandria, The Instructor* 2, 2, eds. Alexander Roberts and James Donaldson, The Ante-Nicene Fathers (Grand Rapids,1979), vol. 2, p. 243.

given to wine..." The Greek word translated by the statement *"not given to wine"* is the word *paroinos* which literally means, 'staying near wine.' It is made up of two words; first *para*, which means 'near to or beside', and *oinos* the common generic Greek word for wine.

When *"not"* is added the meaning is clear: 'not near wine.' The ancient Greek person who was called a *paroinos* was known for attending drinking parties. But church leaders should be known for avoiding drinking parties. These are gatherings expressly organised with the purpose of drinking alcohol.

The Constitutions of the Holy Apostles is an eight volume work, dated to the Fourth Century AD, with many portions from earlier centuries which contain instruction for church order, especially guidance for those in the ministry. Although it is not authoritative it reveals the practice of the church in its early years before worldliness broke up godly principles: "If any one of the clergy be taken eating in a tavern, let him be suspended, excepting when he is forced to bait at an inn upon the road." [13]

This simply upholds the wise counsel of such scriptures as Proverbs 23:20, *"Be not among winebibbers; among riotous eaters of flesh:"* Socialising in such environments is forbidden to leaders. While we understand that evangelism will invade such environments with the good news of the Gospel, and that sinners who are known for their drinking habits will gather unto such messengers seeking for salvation, Timothy is to appoint elders who stay clear from such social environments where drink is consumed and where they actively participate in them.

Paul repeats this instruction when writing to Titus in chapter 1:7. He says, *"For a bishop must be blameless, as the steward of God; not self-willed, not soon angry, not given to wine..."* Socialising in such environments is comparable to self-will and anger in a leader. They are stubborn acts. We might as well laugh off or make light of anger in a leader if we make light of one who likes to socialise in drinking environments—even if they do not get drunk.

---

[13] *Constitutions of the Holy Apostles* 54, eds. Alexander Roberts and James Donaldson, The Ante-Nicene Fathers (Grand Rapids, 1970), vol. 7, p. 503.

Again in verse eight, Paul gives instructions for the appointment of deacons who had a practical ministry in and to the church: *"Likewise must the deacons be grave, not doubletongued, not given to much wine..."* Although deaconship is not a spiritual leadership position, their character and conduct is also vital to the spiritual welfare of the church.

Older ladies in the church are also instructed in the same manner as the deacons: *"The aged women likewise, that they be in behaviour as becometh holiness, not false accusers, not given to much wine, teachers of good things"* (2:3).

Pro-drinkers have noted, focused upon and emphasised the word *"much"* in this qualification. From this they teach that deacons are being instructed to not drink 'too much' alcoholic wine. They believe this is a call to moderation for deacons and for all believers. They suppose that this is clear evidence that believers are allowed to drink alcoholic wine as long as it is in moderate amounts. But we know from the full scope of our studies, from multiple angles, that **drinking alcohol is never commended even in moderation.**

As we have already seen Elders were to be abstainers from alcoholic wine as were all older men and women. We cannot possibly think that all older men are given a more stringent command than the deacons. When abstinence is understood, practised and taught to the local church by local leaders, it generally pervades the whole church. In such settings the issue of abstinence for deacons is a settled issue. Paul and Timothy need only address the issue of drinking non-alcoholic wine in moderation.

Also, in I Timothy 3:11, the wives of deacons are to abstain from wine just as the elders were instructed. We cannot expect that the deacons have a looser requirement than their own wives. There can be no doubt that deacons are expected to be abstainers like their own wives and the elders. But added to this is a further teaching on moderation.

The deacons are now being exhorted to moderation in drinking 'unfermented' wine. This is **moderation in a good thing.** It is moderation in an allowable thing. A man who is known for over-indulgence in a good and allowable thing, like wine (grape juice), is not suitable to be appointed as a deacon.

We will see a parallel to this if we look at honey. Proverbs 24:13 says, *"My son, eat thou honey, because it is good."* But in 25:16 it says, *"Hast thou found honey? eat so much as is sufficient for thee, lest thou be filled therewith, and vomit it."* And again in verse 27 we are told: *"It is not good to eat much honey:"* Honey is good but *"much"* honey is not. Here are commands to eat honey, but only a sufficient amount. The term *"much"*, is used here to infer moderation in a good thing.

Not only does Scripture give clear instruction concerning the use of alcoholic wine but it also gives clear instructions concerning grape juice. It not only bans the consumption of alcohol but also bans the consumption of too much grape juice.

The third qualification to affect leaders in Paul's teaching concerning alcohol is that *"A bishop then must be...sober..."* (3:2; Tit.1:8). This Greek word is elsewhere translated as *"temperate"* (Tit.2:2) *"discreet"* (v5) and *"sober minded"* (Tit.2:6). It means to be 'sound or whole in mind' and to be self-controlled as a state of mind.

As related earlier in Chapter Three, even one glass of wine or pint of beer is enough to start undermining the natural mental alertness which God has granted to us. Leaders are to guard this gift from any influence or substance that would undermine it. A lessening of the mental faculty, the ability to rightly respond or the ability to weigh and judge situations is not at all acceptable for godly leaders.

Sobriety of the mental facilities necessitates abstinence from any intoxicating influence. A leader who seeks to relax, recuperate, get happy, and forget his troubles or to experience joy through alcoholic drinks has compromised this call to sobriety of mind.

Adherence to these three instructions concerning wine and alcohol are as important as the ability to teach in qualifying true leadership. You can be sure that when church leadership relaxes on this one issue it will affect many other issues and in turn affect the whole church. Nowhere does God commend leaders who practise social drinking or who personally get tipsy by means of alcohol. He utterly condemns it at every turn.

Contemporary Leadership
The only reason we have such a growing problem with social drinking and drunkenness in the Church of our day, is because leaders are setting the standard by their own example. I have watched very carefully as this trend has spread in various church groups in various nations within my own lifetime.
Let me give you an example from contemporary leadership. Mark Driscoll is a popular leader in certain church circles, and holds a wide influence through his teaching and written work. Sadly, he is representative of a number of other leaders.
In his book *Radical Reformission,* published in 2004, he stated:
> "After I entered the ministry as a man of legal drinking age, the drum was again repeatedly beaten for me by well-meaning older pastors. So I never drank alcohol until I was thirty years of age. About that time, I was studying the Scriptures for a sermon about Jesus' first miracle of turning water into wine, as reported in John's gospel, a miracle that Jesus performed when he was about my age. My Bible study convicted me of my sin of abstinence from alcohol. So in repentance I drank a hard cider over lunch with our worship pastor."[14]

Here Driscoll says he was 'convicted' for abstaining, and then goes on to call his previous abstinence from alcohol 'sin.' His form of 'repentance' which followed instantly on the heels of this new insight took the form of drinking alcohol with his worship leader. This is indeed a strange way of interpreting the biblical terms: conviction, sin and repentance.

In order to defend his conduct and his promotion of social drinking, Driscoll, presently continues to promote Kenneth Gentry's book *God Gave Wine* (2001), on his website as, "the most balanced and biblical treatment" that he has seen. A new wave of worldly leaders use this book and its arguments

---

[14] p.146, *Radical Reformission,* Mark Driscoll

as their main doctrinal defence thereby covering their own alcoholic indulgence.

Mark Driscoll, wrote the Foreword to Darrin Patrick's book, *Church Planter*, (August 2010). When dealing with the leadership qualification concerning *"not given to wine"*, Patrick states, "As I coach and mentor church planters and pastors, I am shocked at the number of them who are either addicted or headed toward addiction to alcohol."[15] As an example he mentions one pastor who could not relax after work without several beers.

Alarmingly this is not an isolated or unique case but is a growing trend in different movements and denominations across the western world. They teach moderation but very often so-called **liberty becomes license to sin**. This new breed of leaders has been raised up in a vacuum. The church is suffering from a lack of genuine, Christ-centred, Bible-based and Spirit-filled leadership, not to mention a holy leadership with strong biblical convictions and a tender conscience.

This reveals the rising problem of alcohol dependence and addiction in those circles which have made light of abstinence and in fact treated it as a joke. If such a problem is spreading amongst the leaders of such groups we can only imagine what must be happening amongst the rank and file members especially the young. It is very evident that their doctrine of moderation is not working.

Such leaders who are in bondage to alcohol will have little liberty in preaching against the abuse of alcohol and other sins unless they choose to be hypocritical preachers. How can such leaders be used by God to bring deliverance to those whose lives have been ruined by alcoholism? These leaders are now part of the problem instead of part of the cure.

A casual approach to such things as alcohol always produces terrible fruit. The Bible warns that alcohol is like a serpent's bite but many preachers and leaders today take delight in mocking those who take heed to the serious God-given warnings of Scripture.

Another so-called classic defence of social drinking is the book, *Drinking with Calvin and Luther* (2003), by Pastor Jim

---

[15] p.51, *Church Planter,* Darrin Patrick

West, with a Foreword by R.C. Sproul Jr. This book uses "humour and wit" throughout. From its contents, manner and style as well as its popularity it would seem that "foolish talking", (silly talk or buffoonery) as well as "jesting", (witticism, ribaldry, well-turned repartee) are now the means to defend the cause of social drinking as the right and liberty of every Christian (Eph.5:4).

I do not consider this a biblical or honourable way to treat such a serious and vital subject especially when social drinking is doing so much harm in such circles particularly with those in ministry, not to mention rank and file church members.

Jim West does not stop with such jesting. Periodically in his book he insinuates that to disagree or oppose the right and liberty of the social drinker is mere 'Pharasaism' and 'legalism.' He describes such opposition as a 'holier than thou' attitude and warns that such have 'unwittingly' joined the ranks of those who have departed from the faith. All of this is veiled with humorous history and some so-called biblical arguments. It would seem that the prime ethos of his book is that man's chief end is to enjoy wine!

This is a tragic veneer covering a judgement, a plague and an apostasy which is visiting the leadership of the contemporary Church. They accuse those who do not follow their example and teaching of legalism and apostasy, yet they are acting in a manner which is a direct departure from the practice of New Testament leadership.

In the midst of this drinking epidemic there is a serious lack of taking the written Scriptures seriously, for they do not warn or remove from ministry those who continue in such an alcoholic dependent condition. Eli was a good, godly man, who walked uprightly and rebuked the sin of his sons but he would not remove them from ministry, so he was judged of God.

Leaders who feel the need to turn to drink in order to relax, to cope with life, to deal with pressure or to sleep at night are not only unsuitable for public ministry—they are on a dangerous slippery slope. Wine is never suggested in God's Word as an answer or help for these problems.

Such so-called leaders should first get out of ministry and secondly get back to a relationship with Jesus Christ in which true fellowship with Him shall become their true source, sustenance, satisfaction and supply, rather than alcohol.

I am fully aware that there will be some very sincere upright leaders who believe in social drinking but this does not make it right or acceptable. You will remember that when David used a Philistine cart to bring the Ark of the Covenant to the temple in Jerusalem, it was with a pure motive and a genuine heart, yet God rejected this by striking Uzzah dead. Uzzah stretching forth his hand was the result of not acting according to the Word of God and the order of God.

David initially blazed with anger as a result of God's judgement in rejecting something he had done with a right heart and motive. He was only preserved by his fear of the Lord which turned his heart back to inquire of the biblical manner by which the Ark was to be returned which they then carefully followed with great success (II Sam.6).

It is time for leaders to wake up and realise that many Uzzah's are being struck down on the left and the right. But the cause is not the ox that shakes the cart, or the Uzzah who desires to steady it, it is the fact that the methodology is utterly wrong and rejects the written order and pattern of God. It does not matter how perfect your motive, how right the cause or whether you have a heart like King David, the Lord has rejected social drinking amongst His leaders and church. No exception.

CHAPTER 7
SOCIAL DRINKING AMONGST GOD'S PEOPLE

By 'social drinking', we generally mean Christians who drink alcoholic wine or beer but who do not get drunk in a manner that causes them to sway when they walk or slur when they speak. Many today think that by stopping short of intoxication or drunkenness they have the full backing and support of God and of the Bible. But do they? That is our next question. Does God's Word encourage or even allow Christians to drink alcohol?

In recent decades the practice of social drinking has swept the church. Alongside this we have seen biblical standards fall on all fronts. Dress code, separation from the world, purity in the pulpit, the centrality of Christ, the written Word of God, the Blood, the Cross, and a host of other foundational truths have been side-lined. Truth has been sacrificed on the altar of carnal desire.

The fact that amongst the churches of this generation there has been a mass turning toward social drinking is a symptom of something far worse. **A militant promotion of social drinking has always been a symptom of a departure from God, holy convictions and the ancient paths of truth.**

A backslidden people will be sent prophets who will begin to prophesy that they *should* drink wine and strong drink, and a backslidden people will receive such a message and messenger. *"If a man walking in the spirit and falsehood do lie, saying, I will prophesy unto thee of wine and of strong drink; he shall even be the prophet of this people"* (Micah 2:11).

A prophet who prophesies of such things is called a liar. This prophet is walking in a spirit of falsehood. His whole being is motivated by untruth, sham and deceit. The people in Micah's day were in such a terrible state spiritually, that they would receive such a prophet if he came prophesying about the consumption of alcohol.

The calling and ministry of a prophet is not to commend alcohol but to reveal the mind of God in bringing the people back to repentance. There is something wrong when national prophets promote wine and strong drink but have lost a message of heart repentance and obedience.

Such a similar turning from God happened in Amos' day. He was a pure young man whom God called and gifted to be a prophet to a backslidden religious system. In chapter 2:8 he says that they *"drink the wine of the condemned in the house of their god."* The same wine which was condemning godless men to Hell for drunkenness was being drunk by these so-called leaders and followers of the true God.

This same religious system was enjoying great financial prosperity and forsaking any teaching concerning coming judgment. They believed that they were in the midst of one of the greatest of revivals. It was a worship revival in which they talked much about personal anointing but side-lined any talk of affliction. They rebuked leaders who dealt with sin and commanded true prophets to stop prophesying.

But that is not all. In 2:12 they *"gave the Nazarites wine to drink."* Holy young men who wanted to separate themselves from every influence of this world and to yield themselves totally to a pursuit of God were given wine to drink by this new revival. It was an hour when leaders made fun of those who sought separation from wine in order to walk with God.

In Amos 4:1, he says, *"Hear this word, ye kine of Bashan, that are in the mountain of Samaria...which say to their masters, Bring, and let us drink."* This so-called revival was filled with the world, living in the world, like the world. The people were so carnal that they called unto their leaders to bring them drink. In 6:6, we read that even a part of their gathering together was for the purpose to *"drink wine in bowls."*

This demand for drink is preached as a liberty, an allowance and a 'right' by the backslidden. When preachers give themselves over to protect the act of social-drinking rather than strongly warning of the dangers of lusting after it and of demanding it, we know we have reached a dark hour.

Amos' day is exactly like our own; the act, practice and doctrine of indulgence in alcoholic drink is forcibly and strongly promoted, practiced and taught right in the very House of God without shame or conviction.

This is only one example of the popularity of drinking alcohol in the midst of God's people; a people who think they are in revival yet remain intact, living like the world. No wonder there is great numerical growth at such times.

Young Amos prophesied against this thirst, lust and desire for wine and strong drink as did every true Old Testament Prophet. Only false prophets prophesy to the church that they can drink wine and strong drink and yet please God and walk with Him.

An emphasis on drinking alcoholic wine only arose in ancient Israel when she was backslidden. No good fruit ever came from this practice. Search out every righteous man in the Old Testament who indulged in this sin and you read of terrible consequences even though they repented and returned to God.

Social Drinking in the New Testament

I Peter 4:3-4, *"For the time past of our life...when we walked in lasciviousness, lusts, excess of wine, revellings, banquetings, and abominable idolatries: Wherein they think it strange that ye run not with them to the same excess of riot, speaking evil of you:"*

Peter here speaks of many of the activities of believers before their conversion and the fact that now they no longer participate in these things. Because of their rejection of these pursuits they are thought *"strange"* and *"spoken evil of"* by the world and all who enjoy such things.

Three of the things he mentions—*"excess of wine, revellings"* and *"banqueting"*—relate to wine and alcohol so we shall investigate these three terms in order to gain a full picture of exactly what practices of society were not allowed to enter the lifestyle of true believers who made up the early Church.

The first of these pursuits was *"excess of wine."* The word *oinophlugia* which is used here is made up of two words: *oinos,* which is our word for wine, and *phluaros,* meaning to *bubble up.* This is distinct and different from the normal Greek word *methe,* used for the act of repeated or habitual drunkenness. It would seem to denote a state between soberness and drunkenness, but no doubt closer to drunkenness.

It is a state of not-quite-full inebriation but a state in which the alcohol is evident and taking affect. This probably speaks of a man who can hold his drink. He has consumed much but the worst traits of intoxication are not evident; evidence such as slurred speech and a staggering walk. Because of this he deceives himself in thinking that all is 'ok' because he is not drunk.

It is an act of the unregenerate (unsaved) but most certainly not of the saved man or woman. Those who try to walk close to the line by indulging in alcohol and its affects are deceiving themselves. They pride themselves on not being drunkards, or addicted or dependent on the taste, aroma and affects of alcohol, yet this state is condemned by God's Word just as much as drunkenness itself.

There is something terribly wrong with a man who wants to walk close to the line. **The Word of God condemns not only drunkenness, but the stages before drunkenness; not only full intoxication but that pathway which leads to it.** Those who desire and seek the effect of intoxication without being intoxicated are playing games.

Such scriptures as that written by Peter reveal that the early church was not at all an imitator of the world but separate from it. It is popular in our day to hear so-called leaders promoting the imitation of the world in order to reach it with the Gospel, but such things are condemned by God's Word.

Peter also mentions *"revellings"* (*komos*), which when used in the New Testament is always connected and associated with drunkenness but distinct and different from it (Rom.13:13; Gal.5:21). This is a Greek word which was well known and understood in Greek culture and literature.

The *komos* could be a part of any public celebration or event and involved music, singing, dancing, eating, fancy dress, late nights and especially drinking alcohol to create the atmosphere of boisterous merry-making at any public event. It was a party under the influence of alcohol, but most commonly a local village party where those involved drank for entertainment and joy.

The earliest mention of *komos* in Greek literature was as part of wedding festivities. After the wedding or as part of it, a merry and happy party atmosphere was created through drinking wine. By this means natural inhibitions were relaxed and tongues loosened.

This of course is distinct from being drunk or even half way to a state of drunkenness. It is when the individual is in a relaxed, happy state through alcohol and then joins with others in the same state to have a party.

There was the modest *komos* which was carried on with an air of respectability but also the immoral *komos* which led to immorality, or promoted the right atmosphere to eventually lead to sexual immorality. At such parties, inhibitions between men and women were relaxed and lost.

The ancient practice and now the new contemporary practice of introducing alcohol at the festivities of weddings, is certainly included in this. Christians are to have nothing to do with this practice. No fermented drink should be served at a Christian wedding to pacify the world or satisfy a compromising church, or those wrongly taught.

Some would have us believe that the wedding at Cana was a drunken party, or at least a wedding festivity heavily influenced by alcohol. But it was no such thing. The early church utterly rejected such a practice.

The conduct and order of *komos* parties were moulded by the influence of alcohol and as a result produced relaxed inhibitions. This is in utter contrast to all Christian gatherings which are always ordered according to the Word of God and are heavily influenced by the Holy Spirit.

The *komos* was the invention of that religion which worshipped the wine god Bacchus. It most certainly does not come from the teachings and practice of the churches raised up by the Apostles.

It is thought that our English word *comedy* may even be derived from *komos*. This is an hour in the church when everything is made light. Everything is a joke. Social drinking certainly helps this state of affairs. Holiness and purity are laughed at as narrow, old fashioned and legalistic while social drinking is applauded and given a place of high esteem, respect—a special untouchable status.

The third word Peter uses which is associated with wine and alcohol is *"banqueting" (potos)*. This word in no way refers to what we think of as a banquet. This was not a gathering in order to eat. It was a gathering for the specific purpose of drinking together. The binding activity was the drinking of alcoholic wine. It was a drinking party.

It did not necessarily lead to drunkenness but it gave such an opportunity and easily led to such. *Potos* literally means 'a drinking.' Of course drinking in itself is not wrong but if the substance drunk is condemned in the Bible, then that act of drinking is condemned. The ancient *potos* was a gathering together to drink alcoholic drinks and was condemned by the early Church.

At the time that the Bible was translated into English, the term *banquet* was regularly used and well understood in English society. After a group of friends had finished a meal together in a home, they would retire to a private room where they would be served sweet, spiced wine and distilled spirits. This was called the banquet. William Shakespeare (1564-1616), used it in thirteen of his plays in this sense. The translators of the English Bible were not ignorant of this.

The ancient *potos* is synonymous with contemporary gatherings for wine tasting, cocktail parties, church gatherings which entice people with the offer of drinking alcohol, and other specific events when alcohol consumption is the activity that draws the people together. Sadly such events are now celebrated by those calling themselves Evangelical Christians.

The early Church was to keep itself from all sorts of habits connected to the drinking of fermented wine which were common in the secular society around them. Peter states clearly that those in the 'world' thought true believers were strange for not participating in these things. This practice of abstinence was totally foreign to the thinking of the world and was considered an unusual entertaining spectacle to their sight.

As a result he says, 'they speak evil of you.' This is still the common response to those who abstain from such practices. Sadly today the ridicule often comes from within the Church, from those professing to love Jesus Christ, and from leaders who should know better.

Social Drinking in the Contemporary Church

I am very aware that there are genuine believers who in sincerity believe a casual occasional drink is 'ok for a Christian', and who consider themselves very careful in the moderate consumption of alcohol. Such sincere believers would never consider drawing an abstainer into drinking alcohol, and would never mock or make light of those who do abstain. However this is certainly not the norm.

I have heard the same story over and over again, from younger broken and grieved believers who have repeatedly come under immense pressure to drink alcohol from so-called mature Christians in local churches. Since the year, 2000, I have come across this same scenario in many different nations.

This is not an occasional incident pushed by some extreme group. It is a trend, an ingrained doctrine, and established practice across a wide variety of denominational groups from the leadership straight through to every level of ministry and age group.

I have spoken with a number of those who have come through *Teen Challenge* or some other rehabilitation centre or programme, whom upon leaving such an environment and settling into a local church, have immediately been confronted by the pressure to drink alcohol—by those in the local church.

When they turn down the initial advance they are informed that such an attitude is legalistic and are told that because they are under Grace, they have the right to drink alcohol in moderation. After a period of consistent pressure, watching leaders and mature believers drink, they turn back to the very thing that once bound them.

While in the midst of writing this very chapter, I received yet another email that followed this same pattern. This young lady had read my article online and as a result emailed me:

> "When I was first saved the hardest thing for me was giving up my red wine. I managed to do so for two years and then fell into the compromise of the church of saying as long as I didn't get drunk it was fine. Well no matter what, I always ended up crossing the line and found myself almost addicted once more. I gave it up over and over but it was a true stronghold. I am so glad I ran across this article and that it has now confirmed what the Lord has been teaching me. God bless you and please pray for me for my continual surrender to the Lord in this area…The church truly does need your book. This epidemic is huge within the church…the church did make it hard when I would seek advice from leaders and they all said the same thing; that its sin for some and not others, depending on how much a stronghold it was in your life before Christ. That never truly sat well with me, so after much conviction I surrendered and have been searching the scriptures myself for answers."

Tragically, this young lady is not a one-off case. A whole generation of young believers has become a target for the moderation doctrine. The pro-drinkers flaunt their so-called liberty at the expense of the tender convictions of young believers. They mockingly denounce abstinence, temperance and sobriety, as legalism.

All of this reveals that there is an older generation in the church who have grown up under a doctrine of moderation who have been taught the 'one-wine theory', who have little wisdom, concern, love, knowledge, understanding or Holy Spirit-conviction concerning protecting, warning and teaching a new generation about the dangers that face them. Instead of protecting these new believers, they are tearing down their God-given convictions.

At the end of 2012, a story was reported in a Swedish publication concerning a lady called, Mia, who was raised in a Pentecostal home in Sweden. At a young age she gave her life to Jesus Christ. At 13 she was baptized in water. Throughout her teens she was active in church and a bit of a 'home bird'. In 1994 she married, Stefan, a devout follower of Christ. Over the next few years they had three kids. After having moved from a Pentecostal church that taught abstinence to a Charismatic congregation which didn't, Mia attended a friend's birthday party at which several members of the church drank beer and wine. She was surprised at this and thought it strange but the second time drinks were passed around, she decided to have just one. This one drink made her feel happy and free.

After this she secretly went out and bought a bottle with the desire to experience the same feelings. She drank it while her husband was on night duty. This led to her frequenting pubs, distancing herself from church meetings, and finally getting involved in an adulterous relationship. It wrecked her marriage and ultimately led to divorce. Thankfully though, by God's grace, she repented and was restored to the Lord in 2011, which led to a restoration of the marriage.

This is not a unique story—it has been repeated times without number. The practice of social drinking within the church has done untold damage to a great many in recent decades and no one seems to care.

Drinking alcohol moderately with the approval of the broad Christian world, has led many to a state of dependence on this dangerous, addictive and deceptive poison. Many social drinkers in the church have a serious problem with dependence on alcohol but do not realize that they depend upon it, or they simply do not want to admit it.

It is stated in one medical report that: "The hallmark of dependence is an inability to refrain from taking alcohol without experiencing psychological and/or physical discomfort." **Dependence does not mean that you cannot refrain from it but that it is hard to refrain.**

Dependence is just another word for addiction. If you depend upon alcohol for joy, peace, sleep, or as a source for some other mood which will help you cope with life then it is an addiction. **Many are addicted who are sure in their own minds that they are not drunkards and never could be.**

Dependence upon a drug (even a popular drug) which has the innate ability to undermine your God-given faculties, and has the potential for addiction, is dangerous. Those who ignore this are walking on thin ice. The medical profession has consistently warned that 10% of those who taste alcohol will become alcoholics.

Regular social drinkers are able to gradually take larger amounts of alcohol over a period of years but maintain what they think is the same safe limit of influence. The human body develops a certain tolerance to alcohol. As a result more is needed in order to reach the same effects which were previously enjoyed. Alcohol slowly and deceitfully draws the drinker in deeper.

We now live in a generation where it is the custom for church-goers to teach their children the so-called good virtue of treating alcohol with respect. They think that if they teach their children at an early stage to drink moderately and in a responsible fashion within the family environment, all will be 'ok'. Sadly many parents have realized far too late that they have cursed their children and grandchildren with this addictive habit. It is like placing a young person on the back of an unbroken wild stallion.

Mr. Arthur Guinness (1724–1803), of Ireland, who founded the famous (or should we say infamous?) brewery was actually a believer in Christ who sat under John Wesley's ministry in Dublin. He was utterly against any form of intoxication, but not against drinking beer moderately. Starting with a small brewery in 1752, he took his personal home-made stout recipe and under the motto "My hope is in God," started his brewery business.

During the 1760s, he started his meteoric rise to fame and fortune. He also went on a militant campaign against Whiskey and other distilled spirits which were destroying the country, and spoke out strongly against all forms of intoxication.

He naively thought his brew was a safe alternative to aid the people of Ireland by steering them into a healthier way of life, free from drunkenness. However, Arthur Guinness lived long enough to dismiss four of his grandchildren from the brewery for drunkenness and related problems.

A new secular anti-alcohol campaign states that:

> "In Northern Ireland over half of young people aged between 11 and 16 say they've had an alcoholic drink at some point in their lives." It goes on to clearly state: "Some parents may feel that giving their child a small amount of alcohol in their early teens will give them a responsible attitude to alcohol, but there is no scientific evidence to support this. In fact, **research shows that the earlier a child starts drinking, the higher his or her risk of serious alcohol-related problems later in life**…Children often copy what their parents do and how they act. What you do may influence your child as much as what you say. It may be useful to think about your own relationship with alcohol and what messages it could be sending to your child. Think about your own drinking habits, even if you aren't a heavy drinker."

The doctrine of social drinking cares more about its own rights than the health of the Church. It is sacrificing a young generation who have grown up in Christian families as well as a whole generation of new converts in the fires of Molech, and on the altars of Bacchus (Lev.18:1; 20:2-5; I Kgs.11:7; II Kgs.23:10; Jer.32:35-36). We are sowing the wind in these young lives and we will reap a whirlwind of tragedy across the Church in the next decades unless the Lord sends a wonderful genuine revival to recover His testimony (Hos.8:7).

Because of the innate dangers in alcohol, the strongest warnings should be coming from the pulpits of those movements and churches which teach the moderation doctrine. If the leaders who teach that social drinking is biblically allowed are genuinely sincere (even if sincerely wrong) then they should be warning more strongly and pointedly than any abstainer. Yet this is not the case.

Many churches in our generation have chosen to coexist and even strongly promote a potentially dangerous, lethal and addictive drug which is destructive to the mental, physical, social and spiritual good of every individual. In these very same churches there is more made of defending dependence upon alcohol than warnings against it.

While the early Church separated from all forms of social drinking which were common in secular society, our contemporary Church is pursuing after these practices, imitating the world. In a fresh return to the practice of the early Church there will be a fresh return to abstinence which will include a rejection of social drinking as well as drunkenness.

CHAPTER 8
SOBER SAINTS

There are constant exhortations in the Bible for the Christian to be *sober*. This is not an optional piece of advice or a suggestion; it is a clear warning and a pointed command. The Christian's life is to be marked by sobriety. The Christian's walk is also to be continually protected by the same sobriety.

There are five different Greek words in the New Testament which are used to speak of sobriety. One of them is the Greek word *nepho*, which as we saw in the section on New Testament Leadership, is normally translated into English as *sober*, (although the word *watch* is used as well) but which can be literally translated as 'to be free from the influence of intoxicating drinks' or 'to abstain from wine.' Those who are *nepho*, do not drink wine.

The other four words for *sober* have a wider application but all of them still have a direct bearing on the influence of wine upon the mind of a believer.

As we have already seen the Jewish historian Josephus, who lived in Rome, and the Jewish philosopher, Philo, who lived in Alexander, both defined *nepho* in their writings as specifically abstinence from alcoholic wine. Both of these men lived at opposite ends of the Roman Empire during the First Century when the New Testament Scriptures were written. We could also fill pages with quotes from other ancient authors who lived before, during and after Christ who used the '*nepho* word group' numbers of times in reference to abstaining from fermented wine and other alcoholic drinks.

This verifies that *nepho,* was a generally understood and widely used term in the Greek language within the Roman Empire for total abstinence from any drink that would make a man drunk. This not only covered wine but any intoxicating drink.

W.E. Vine, in his very popular, *Expository Dictionary of Old and New Testament Words,* also distinctly defines the word *nepho* (sober) as: "to be free from the influence of intoxicants."

But this by itself is not sufficient evidence for us. We must look to the writers of Scripture in the First Century to see how the Church understood it. As we do, we shall see that Paul and Peter are in full agreement with each other and with the simple fact that *nepho* meant **abstinence from alcoholic drinks**.

This word *nepho* is mentioned six times in our New Testament and was used by the Apostles to instruct the churches concerning their lifestyle. Let us take the six mentions of this word and study them in the New Testament.

Paul

Paul mentions it twice when he writes to the Church at Thessalonica: *"Ye are all the children of light, and the children of the day: we are not of the night, nor of darkness. Therefore let us not sleep, as do others; but let us watch and be sober* [**nepho**]. *For they that sleep, sleep in the night; and they that be drunken are drunken in the night. But let us, who are of the day, be sober* [**nepho**] *putting on the breastplate of faith and love; and for an helmet, the hope of salvation"* (I Thess.5:5-8).

Drunkenness is contrasted with soberness—they are opposites. This clearly reveals that the soberness mentioned in these scriptures is specifically that of abstaining from alcohol.

Here, Paul speaks of the Christian life. The cure for sleep is watchfulness, and the cure for the sin of drunkenness is sobriety—abstinence. You cannot be both sober and drunk at the same time. You must be one or the other. If you do not want to cross the line and fall into the sin of drunkenness then just do not drink alcohol!

These scriptures show clearly that the act of drunkenness is a thing of *darkness*. 'Night' in these scriptures represents the lifestyle and actions of those in the world who do not know Jesus Christ as Lord and Saviour. Paul twice calls this church to sobriety by saying *"Let us...be sober."*

By this he says let all those who are children of light, children of the day, true Christians, *"be sober."* If you are a true Christian then be sober, abstain from wine; do not come under any influence of intoxication from wine. He does not advise moderation in connection with alcohol, he exhorts to abstinence. **The only alternative offered in the Bible for drunkenness is total abstinence.**

He goes on to say that a Christian maintains sobriety by putting on the armour of God. The only way to fight this Christian war against Satan, the world and the flesh is by being sober. Anyone who leaves the sure and safe shoreline of sobriety is opening the door for these three traditional enemies of Adam's race to gain entrance.

The only way to protect oneself from the enemy is to be sober. The armour mentioned here is *"the breastplate of faith and love; and for an helmet, the hope of salvation."* Faith, love and hope, are the attributes of soberness, not of drunkenness. Only the sober put on such armour.

Drunkenness will undermine these three great Christian attributes and the Enemy will have his desired breach for attack. If a man embraces social drinking and goes on to cross the line numerous times, the Devil can come and attack his mind with doubts over his salvation. He will be condemned by the accusation of his enemy.

Concerning this breastplate it is elsewhere called a *breastplate of righteousness*. The love and faith referred to specifically point to a holiness of life which protects the heart of a believer from fainting. Sobriety is a great aid to putting on this breastplate through faith and love. Drunkenness is an utter enemy to holiness and purity of heart.

Decide for yourself what helps holiness of heart and life most: drunkenness or sobriety, abstinence or social drinking? Does social drinking aid holiness? Does it help towards a solid and assured hope of salvation? These are questions you must answer for yourself.

The second place Paul, talks about this same soberness, is in his second letter to young Timothy.

II Tim.4:2-5, *"Preach the word; be instant in season, out of season; reprove, rebuke, exhort with all longsuffering and doctrine. For the time will come when they will not endure sound doctrine; but after their own lusts shall they heap to themselves teachers, having itching ears; And they shall turn away their ears from the truth, and shall be turned unto fables. But watch [**nepho**] thou in all things, endure afflictions, do the work of an evangelist, make full proof of thy ministry."*

This is good instruction to a young preacher involved heavily in full-time ministry. But take note of the conditions that face him in his future ministry. An hour of apostasy lies ahead for him in which so-called Christians who say that they believe in Jesus, the Cross, the love of God, and the blessings of God, will begin to tire of sound preaching from the Bible—especially if it involves the reproving and rebuking of sin. A rebellion will rise against the written Word of God.

He warns Timothy that they will not endure healthy biblical teaching and preaching but will mould the message to suit their own lusts. If a preacher brings a message of liberty and freedom from all biblical limitations and restraints, then they will receive him because it gives room to their own lusts and desires. Such believers will be drawn to fables and false stories, but will turn away their ears from scriptural commands.

It is vital to highlight here what we have already shown: that the doctrine of social drinking is built upon a foundation of several myths. The word *"fables"* (*mythos*) which Paul uses in this passage actually means myths or tales which are fictitious narratives and stories. Paul warns that many will turn from sound doctrine and truth to fables.

Paul then gives clear instruction to young Timothy of what he is to do; *"But watch [**nepho**] thou in all things."* Be sober in all things. Be free from wine or any other influence at all times, in every situation and around all people. Social drinking will not help in the task of preaching truth in a compromising age and generation.

When he says to, *"watch in all things"*, he means while relaxing, when taking breaks and when alone, just as much as when in the pulpit, or dealing with people. We are to be sober at all times, on all occasions in every way possible.

I want to say a word here to those in ministry. Do not be caught up in social drinking, or Leaders' meetings held in pubs or youth meetings held in pubs. Do not be pressed into the mould of the world by a backslidden Church. Preach the Word of God in season and out of season whether it is popular in the Church, or unpopular. Be sober, abstain from alcohol, no matter what the Church or Christians think of you or say about you.

We need a new generation of preachers in the Church who will rise up to be a pattern and example of godliness who will abstain from taking any intoxicating drink and teach the saints and churches to do likewise.

It is so important that young preachers stand their ground, unmovable in such days if they are really going to be spiritually effective and fulfil the ministry God has given them. When the Church begins to slumber and sleep spiritually, and to enter into a lifestyle of social drinking, thereby allowing darkness to enter the Church, the need for preachers of the Word is greater. We need preachers of the person of Christ and preachers of the commands of Christ who will back up their message with a sober life of total abstinence from wine or any alcoholic drink.

Peter

Next we turn to Peter's first Epistle where he uses this word, *sober*, three times. Firstly, he uses it in reference to all the things that the Apostles (who were inspired by the Holy Ghost) had preached and taught in those first churches.

"Wherefore gird up the loins of your mind, be sober [**nepho**] *and hope to the end for the grace that is to be brought unto you at the revelation of Jesus Christ"* (I Pet.1:13).

He instructs them to be sober by girding up the loins of their mind—in other words, to lay hold of every thought and meditation of the mind—like a man in Bible days tucking his garments into his belt that he might run without tripping up.

We are to fasten down every 'floating thought'; all loose thinking in order that we might be sober. Any thinking which leads away from sobriety must be dealt with. Any thinking that will lead you to social drinking must be dealt with. Don't even entertain the thought.

Why should we do this? Only those who are sober in mind and life have the right to truly hope for the grace of God which will be brought to sober saints, when Jesus returns again in glory.

I have heard many try to plead their right and liberty to drink alcohol because they are under Grace, but the scripture above says that only those who are sober will be truly able to hope for God's grace at His return. Who is right?

Again Peter says in chapter four verse seven, *"But the end of all things is at hand: be ye therefore sober, and watch* [**nepho**] *unto prayer."* In the light of us living at the end of time, if we believe it, we will live a sober un-intoxicated lifestyle. Notice that a different word *sober* is here placed before the Greek word we are studying. He is saying be sober, or be of a sound, sane, certain mind and also abstain from wine in order that you may give yourself to prayer. This just proves that the word we are using is specifically pointing to abstaining from wine-drinking and not just a mental sobriety.

In the verses preceding this he speaks of their old life when they walked in *"excess of wine, revellings, banqueting";* when they longed for what was forbidden putting things before God Himself. That is why he calls these Christians (who once lived a life of social drinking, partying and drunkenness) to remember that the end is nigh and to continue walking in sobriety. The answer and correct response to a culture influenced by alcohol and social drinking is total abstinence.

Then the last mention of this word is in 5:8, *"Be sober* [**nepho**] *be vigilant; because your adversary the devil, as a roaring lion, walketh about, seeking whom he may devour:"*

Those who indulge in tipsiness, excessive drinking or social drinking, leave themselves wide open to the advances and strategies of the Devil who seeks to devour every believer. You may know your authority in Christ; you may laugh at the Devil for being toothless but if you do not live in sobriety your life is wide open to the attacks of the Devil. Peter says that Satan seeks whom *"he may devour."* This single word *katapino* literally means 'to drink down.' What he is saying is that Satan is going around as a roaring lion seeking *to drink down* those who drink down fermented wine. Please do not be deceived: **Alcohol is part of the arsenal of Satan against the church.**

There is no point in binding him, preaching against him, or praying for deliverance from him, if you have no desire to abstain from the influence of strong drink. I have often found that those who are determined not to listen to scriptural wisdom but who continue walking close to the line are proud. Pride shuts the ears to wisdom, the heart to knowledge and the mind to understanding. Pride goes before a fall.

The verses preceding this last one exhort us by saying: *"Likewise, ye younger, submit yourselves unto the elder. Yea, all of you be subject one to another, and clothed with humility: for God resisteth the proud, and giveth grace to the humble. Humble yourselves therefore under the mighty hand of God, that he may exalt you in due time:"*

May God give you the grace to be clothed in humility and so to listen to the wisdom of God's Word by living a sober, drink-free life which will honour God and deliver you out of the hand and mouth of the Devil. The days in which we live call for and demand an arising of Sober Saints who will stand their ground, unmovable, unchangeable, who will fight a good fight, preach the truth and wait patiently and soberly for the return of Jesus Christ.

CHAPTER 9
A SPIRIT-FILLED LIFE

"And be not drunk with wine, wherein is excess; but be filled with the Spirit" (Eph.5:18). God's answer to an alcohol influenced life is for a man to be saved, sanctified and Spirit-filled.

In Ephesians chapter five, it is clearly stated that the wine mentioned has in its very nature or intrinsic character, *'excess.'* When it speaks of *'excess'* it is not at all talking about the amount drunk or even about the results of drinking; **it is describing the indwelling character of the actual drink.**

The Greek term *asotia,* used here literally means, 'un-saved-ness' or 'un-savable-ness.' It means the opposite of saved. It is made up of two Greek terms: *sozo* meaning saved; and *'a'* which when added as a prefix, makes the word mean the opposite.

So then *asotia,* is set as the opposite of the term, *sozo* which is widely used in the New Testament for the act of salvation or deliverance when a person is brought to Christ and into Christ. **Mark carefully that the nature and effect of salvation is set in opposition to the nature and effect of alcohol.**

In other words, it is literally saying that the character revealed by an alcoholic drink is in opposition to the character and nature manifested by those who are saved. These two are opposites and can never be reconciled.

Barnes explains, *excess* as meaning: "...that which is unsafe, not to be recovered; lost beyond recovery...that which is abandoned to sensuality and lust; dissoluteness, debauchery, revelry." This is confirmed when the other references where it is used are studied (Tit.1:6; I Pet.4:4; Lk.15; 13).

More specifically, it is saying that built into the nature of alcoholic wine is the tendency to be carried into a lifestyle of conduct and actions which are contrary to a life of salvation in Christ. Paul here makes a clear statement, *"be not drunk with wine."* He then sets forth an alternative filling for the New Testament Christian: *"be filled with the Spirit."*

Just as the command is clear *"be not drunk,"* it is also a clear command to *"be filled with the Holy Spirit."* These two things are compared and contrasted. When filled with alcohol the influence is manifest in the speech, the walk, the attitude, in fact in all things. It speaks of an influence upon the whole life.

This is comparable to the Spirit-filled life. When a man is truly filled with the Holy Spirit every area of his life is affected and influenced by the Holy Spirit. To be filled with the Holy Spirit is to come under the influence or effect of the Holy Spirit. The smallest influence of the work of the Holy Ghost in a life will have a manifest result.

It is impossible to partake of alcohol without it immediately beginning to affect every faculty. It is also impossible to come under the influence of the Holy Spirit without Him immediately affecting various areas of your life. After a time, both will be evident to all.

It is of interest to note two incidents of people wrongly accused of drunkenness. The first is Hannah, in I Samuel chapter one, who was marked out as a righteous lady who poured forth prayers and intercessions unto God for a man-child; a prophet. In verse 13 we are told *"Eli thought she had been drunken."* Here is a woman who is in the hand of God, under the work of the Holy Spirit but is misunderstood and accused of being drunk by a leader.

She responded: *"I have drunk neither wine nor strong drink...Count not thine handmaid for a daughter of Belial:"*

Hannah was clear in understanding that only children of Belial would come under the influence of alcohol. It is worth noting that *"the sons of Eli were sons of Belial"*. Not only did Eli misjudge a prayerful lady for a drunken lady, he also allowed his immoral sons to continue in ministry (I Sam.3).

The second incident is on the day of Pentecost when the Disciples were filled with the Holy Ghost. Some made the accusation that, *"These men are full of new wine."* It was very obvious that these Disciples had come under the strong influence of something which was affecting everything about them.

Please note that drunkenness would have left these Disciples incoherent in coordination, speech and action but instead they were bold, calm, eloquent and convincing. A filling with the true Holy Ghost made them shake off fear and stand up publicly to preach a powerful and convicting message.

Paul also draws a very distinct line between the influence of alcohol and the influence of the Spirit to the believers in Ephesus. These two things are also set in contrast and opposition to each other. It would be an utter contradiction to think of a Christian or a Spirit-filled believer coming under the influence of alcohol in any degree.

A truly Spirit-filled believer ought not to come under any other influence. This is the issue—an issue of influence, effect and control. What influence should be upon the Christian's life to lead and direct him?—only the influence of the Holy Ghost.

Jude tells us in 1:19 *"These be they who separate themselves, sensual, having not the Spirit."* These were people who had mixed with the Church calling themselves Christians and making much of the fact that they had the Spirit and were led by the Spirit. In reality however by their separation from the Apostles, the Apostle's teachings, and other true believers, they revealed that they did not have the true Holy Spirit.

The same goes for those who continually indulge in coming under the intoxicating influence of alcohol; by such actions they reveal that they are not Spirit-filled or Spirit-led. They may claim a profound experience of the Holy Ghost but the Holy Spirit will not indwell and fill a life that will not yield to Him, obey Him and come under His influence and control. The true Holy Spirit will not share His temple with the addictive influence of alcohol.

The remedy for remaining free from the influence of alcohol or any other moulding influence of the world is to *"be filled with the Spirit."* When filled with Him there is no room for other influences. When filled with Him there will be no desire to seek for joy, peace, solitude or deliverance in alcohol.

Those who promote social drinking and even the act of getting tipsy through partaking of alcohol in order to be happy, relaxed, joyful and confident are contradicting Scripture on many fronts. Here are so-called believers looking to alcohol rather than the Holy Ghost to make them happy. This is tragic.

It is very interesting that after dealing with the vital subject of being constantly and continually filled with the Spirit, Paul immediately deals with the relationship of husbands and wives (5:22-33), and then moves on to the relationship between parents and children (6:1-4). This reveals that being filled with the Spirit of God directly and immediately affects the home life.

Sadly, the reverse is true also. When the influence of drink comes upon a father, husband, mother, wife or child the result is manifest in the home with a thousand fruits of unrighteousness and frequently results in broken hearts, broken relationships, broken marriages and broken homes. It is a well known fact that twice as many marriages break up through drink as they do through adultery.

The cure to family heartache and breakup is the Spirit-filled life. It brings the kingdom of God into the home manifested in righteousness, peace and joy. This experience of the believer being filled with the Spirit is the place of true joy, satisfaction, social-enjoyment and rest, not alcohol.

Flesh and Spirit

In Galatians chapter five, Paul draws out a picture for us of the conflict between the Spirit and the flesh. He exhorts believers to, *"Walk in the Spirit, and ye shall not fulfil the lust of the flesh."* Scripture speaks not only of us being born of the Spirit (Jn.3:5-8; Gal.4:29) and living in the Spirit (Rom.8:13) but also walking in the Spirit (Gal.5:25).

This walk speaks of a lifestyle lived in Christ-likeness; the habits, practices, thoughts, words, desires and decisions which make up our whole life. Paul goes on to reveal exactly what the manifestation of the 'flesh' having its way in a life looks like, and what the manifestation of the Holy Spirit having His way in a life looks like.

Just one manifestation of the 'flesh' is *'drunkenness'* whereas one manifestation of the fruit of the Spirit is *'temperance'* which is defined as self-control or the ability to control the appetites, lusts and desires of the flesh. If a man cannot control himself, keep or deny himself in relation to alcohol it is an issue either of salvation or of this battle between flesh and Spirit.

By this we can discern if the 'flesh'—the old fallen Adamic nature—is in control, or if the Holy Spirit of God is in control. There is no confusion here or blurring of the lines. He says if you walk in the Spirit, you will not fulfil the lusts or desires of the flesh.

To walk in the Spirit means to walk by the power of the Spirit. The key to a holy life free from the power and influence of the 'flesh' is found in a dependence upon the power of the Holy Spirit. The key to a life lived free from the influence of alcohol or a need and dependence upon it is the promised power of the Holy Spirit.

Many Christians try to live their Christian life by self effort, their own strength, their own will-power, and then wonder why they experience so much failure and defeat. It is because this life is to be lived in **dependence upon the indwelling Holy Ghost**. The Holy Spirit who first brought us to Christ and into salvation is the same one who keeps us walking uprightly until our final destination.

The true mark of the Christian who is born again is the nine-fold fruit of the Spirit. If he is indwelt by the Spirit then this fruit will grow. Although a definite and radical change comes at the point of salvation there is a steady growth into maturity and conformity to Christ by the indwelling of the Spirit.

In the old fallen nature called *'flesh'* is the lust or desire for *'drunkenness.'* This is the character of the old man or the old nature. The desire to come under the influence of alcohol comes from the flesh. The desire for temperance and abstinence comes from the Holy Spirit. We can immediately discern the flesh when we find a desire for this foreign influence.

Paul goes on to say in chapter five, verse 24, *"And they that are Christ's have crucified the flesh with the affections and lusts."* The old nature that desires the influence, effects and fruit of alcohol must go to the Cross. It must be reckoned dead. It must be crucified. It must be treated violently. How sad that some treat these fleshly desires as a friend and mark of the Christian life.

It is by the power and ability of the Holy Spirit that we put off this old man with its lusts and put on the new man which desires to live godly in Christ Jesus. The Holy Spirit will always be known by His work of practically putting the flesh—with its desires—to death at the Cross.

The real Spirit will always move you, prompt you and empower you to put to death any desire for alcoholic influence in your body, which is His temple. How sad then that those being moved upon by the Holy Spirit to live a life of abstinence are accused of being legalistic. To confuse the sanctifying work of the Holy Spirit for legalism is indeed utter confusion.

Alcohol, Reformation and Revival

A new era began in 1517, when Martin Luther nailed his *95 Theses* to the church door in Wittenberg. Within thirty years of this Europe was utterly transformed. Sadly, there were those who under the banner of the Reformation used the message of *justification by faith* as a guise for their own lusts. These praised drinking as an act of 'gospel freedom' and turned the Grace of God into lasciviousness. A subtle doctrine of enjoying the influence of alcohol, whilst professing a walk with God, was created which was called 'evangelical drinking.'

Luther believed in drinking wine and beer moderately but he denounced these 'evangelical drinkers' for using their liberty to promote vice. He preached strongly and pointedly concerning the dangers of alcohol. The social drinking of alcohol, a carryover from Romanism, continued after the Reformation and was only thrown off slowly like a number of other things. But there were those in the midst of the Reformation who preached total abstinence.

Sebastian Franck, (1499-1543), who served as a Lutheran pastor in Nuremberg, published a treatise in 1528, called *Concerning the Horrible Vice of Drunkenness*. He taught strongly against drunkenness and also called for the abolition of alcohol throughout the German-speaking lands. He believed this should be carried out by preachers through the use of God's Word and Church discipline.

The Anabaptist movement, which was also called the *Radical Reformation,* was birthed in reformation and revival. It had its beginnings in Zurich, Switzerland, during the early years of the Reformation. While Luther led the work of Reformation in Germany, Zwingli led it to the south in Switzerland.

The Anabaptist movement began with new converts who were converted out of Catholicism. A group of young, zealous students and scholars gathered around Zwingli in Zurich to be taught the Word of God. However, by 1522, they were dissatisfied with the extent of the Reformation. They desired to practise and preach the fullness of God's Word. They wanted a total return to the written Scriptures on every issue.

In January 1525, a new work was birthed in a small gathering in a home in Zurich. It was not long until the Spirit of God was poured out in a mighty way upon these hungry hearts. We read of 500 new converts being baptized at this time in rivers around St. Gallen. It carried all the marks of a genuine revival.

As a result, many new scholars, preachers and leaders who loved and cherished the written Word, were raised up of God. Abstinence from intoxicating drinks was just one truth to which they returned and taught in a clear, balanced manner across Europe.

One of Zwingli's young men, Ludwig Haetzer, (1500-1529), was a powerful scholar. In 1525, he published his treatise against the consumption of alcohol called *On Evangelical Drinking*. This was a strong, biblical challenge to those in Saxony and Zurich who praised the act of drinking as a part of their Christian liberty. He went as far as to suggest that those who refused to abstain should be expelled from the Christian community. His influence was later felt in Zurich, Augsburg, Basel, Strasbourg and Constance.

In 1527, the very earliest Anabaptist confession of faith was written up by Michael Sattler, (1490-1527), called the *Seven Articles of Schleitheim*. It included a ban on attending 'winehouses.' Both in his preaching and by his example Sattler stood for total abstinence. In 1560, Zwingli said of the Anabaptists, that they only drank sweet, unfermented cider and water.

During the first 20 years of their history, as they spread out across Europe preaching the Gospel and founding new churches, some 10,000 believers were martyred for their holy life and convictions. They would rather die than loosen their grip on the authority of Scripture, or compromise a holy life.

The preaching, teaching and practice of abstinence, was not confined to the Anabaptists. Leaders within other movements like the Hutterites and Mennonites practised and preached the truth of abstinence. The Hutterites began in Moravia through the leadership of Jacob Hutter (1500-1536), an Anabaptist preacher, and spread quickly all across the Germanic nations. Peter Riedemann, (1506-56), a persecuted preacher of the Hutterite movement, while in prison wrote strongly against people working as Innkeepers, or selling intoxicating drinks. This was later incorporated into the Hutterite confession of faith. Michael Seifensieder, a preacher of the Hutterites, was arrested in January 1536, in Vienna, and finally burned at the stake in March. It was discovered that he was a Hutterite preacher because he refused to drink alcohol in an inn.

Mennonites was the name given to the most biblical Anabaptists in the Netherlands. Menno Simons (1496-1561), founder of the Mennonites and a martyr for the faith, made a strong stand against any use of alcohol. He constantly called believers to sobriety and warned of God's judgement against drunkards. His influence was felt in a powerful way, particularly in Holland and Germany.

In 1547, in Geneva under the leadership of John Calvin (1509-1564), laws were passed to stop friends buying each other drinks, or even inviting each other for drinks. This was aimed at those who were called the *Libertines* who taught that they were liberated through the grace of Christ to drink, dance, attend the theatre and enjoy worldly pleasures. Calvin coined the name *Libertine* from the Roman god of viniculture, *Liber*, who was synonymous with Dionysus and Bacchus. All these worldly activities were banned by law that same year.

Although Calvin did not teach total abstinence, this came about as the direct result and influence of Calvin's mentor, Martin Bucer (1491 –1551), who was seventeen years his senior. Bucer, was an associate of Luther, Zwingli and Calvin, who pastored in Strasbourg for several years before arriving in Geneva, and who later spent the last two years of his life in Cambridge, England, by invitation from, Thomas Cranmer, then Archbishop of Canterbury. Bucer, held strong views on drinking, eating and on denying the flesh, which he taught wherever he went.

The initial and best known Reformers did not practise or teach total abstinence, but there were many who laboured with them and who were taught and raised up under them who most certainly did.

These various movements and teachers spread their influence from Hungary in the east, to Britain in the west. In their wake, in the following century, other movements and leaders arose and preached abstinence from alcohol like the Quakers in England under the prophetic leadership of George Fox (1624-1691). As the influence of the Quakers spread across the British Isles abstinence from alcohol was maintained and taught.

Although many genuine leaders and churches continued in some measure to drink socially, the Lord was restoring the truth of abstinence from alcohol and increasingly spreading this truth through the Gospel to lands far and wide.

Before the Methodist revival came to England in the 18th Century, drunkenness was acknowledged as the national vice of rich and poor, yet beer drinking was considered an English virtue. Gin, ale, beer, spirits and liquors were sold cheaply and on an unbelievable scale to young and old.

All over London, in the 1730s, notices could be seen stating: '*Drunk for 1 penny, Dead drunk for tuppence, Straw for nothing.*' Gin was called 'Mothers Ruin' and this period of time, was called the "Gin Craze."

The Justice Department, ordered an enquiry which revealed shocking facts. There had been a drastic rise in the sale, consumption and consequences of drinking alcohol. Worst hit were mothers and children. Hopelessly addicted mothers gave alcohol to their little children, daily. Daughters were sold into prostitution just to maintain the drinking habits of fathers and mothers. [Joel 3:3 *"And they have cast lots for my people; and have given a boy for an harlot, and sold a girl for wine, that they might drink."*]

Politicians refused to pass any bill to combat this national problem. They argued that there would be riots in the streets but it is more likely that no one wanted to damage the high income collected from alcohol sales.

Mr John Wesley was converted in May 1738, which was the time when the Spirit of God was just beginning to be outpoured upon London and the surrounding region through the ministry of George Whitefield, who was converted in 1735.

In his *Rules of the United Societies,* adopted in 1743, Wesley called upon all members, those who were already converted, as well as those who were seeking salvation, to abstain from "drunkenness, buying or selling spirituous liquors, or drinking them, unless in cases of extreme necessity."[16] One hundred years later Methodist preachers were still calling for such principles to be upheld and to be practised, with special attention concerning abstinence from alcohol.

When Wesley visited Mrs. Fletcher of Madeley, he rebuked her sharply when she offered one of his preachers some wine to drink exclaiming, "What! Madam, do you intend to kill my preachers?"[17] He considered fermented wine to be poison and only fit for throwing away. He was utterly against any influence that would weaken or undermine the senses, reason or mind not only spirits but fermented wine as well.

Following close behind Wesley were an army of men who took a strong stance against any use of alcohol. Adam Clarke (1760-1832) the great commentator, Francis Asbury (1745-1816) the pioneer to America, Thomas Cook (1747-1814) the father of Methodist missions, and Hugh Bourne (1772-1852)

---

[16] p.1, *Drink,* G.T. Brake
[17] Ibid

founder of the Primitive Methodists (founded in 1807), all made a clear stand against drinking alcohol; some of them with great militancy.

The early Methodist preachers in England, Wales and Ireland carved a pathway through towns and cities leaving hundreds and thousands of new converts behind them who continued to uphold total abstinence as a part of their new life in Christ and as a part of practical holiness. In the 18th and 19th centuries these revival pioneers carried this message to other Nations and Continents including North America.

Christmas Evans, (1766-1838), the powerful Baptist Gospel preacher, and Welsh Revivalist (frequently called the Spurgeon of Wales) preached total abstinence and would not tolerate the use of intoxicating wine at communion. During the 1830s, he waged a virtual campaign of war against the devilish influence of alcohol in the land with special attention placed upon ministers who protected the act of social drinking. This call to abstinence preceded the great revival of 1839.

One of the remarkable things about the 1859 revival in Wales was the disappearance of widespread drunkenness in secular society. The most noted drunkards in each community were converted and then confirmed their refusal to touch a drop more by joining total abstinence societies. Over the next decades the Lord prepared the main leaders who would be used in future revivals and almost all of them preached abstinence clearly and powerfully.

When the great Welsh revival of 1904 came, the leaders held strong abstinence convictions and the Spirit of God swept the valleys delivering multitudes not only from sin, but from the sin of intoxication. Most of the leaders of this revival were also leaders in the national temperance movement. In Cardiff city police reported that drunkenness dropped by 60% within one month of the beginning of the revival.

As a result of the 1859 and 1904 revivals Baptist, Congregational, Calvinistic Methodists and various free churches stopped using fermented wine at communion, called all members to total abstinence and advised all new converts to sign the *temperance pledge*.

Before the 1859 revival in Ulster (Northern Ireland), drunkenness was a prevalent vice. Rioting and drunkenness were the order of the day. The use of distilled spirits was a widespread curse. The temperance movement, although doing much good, made little impact in the land. But in that wonderful year of 1859, 100,000 souls turned to Christ for salvation. The Countess of Londonderry noted that the revival resulted in the closing of public houses (bars) and the establishment of greater soberness and temperance. One politician noted the dramatic and radical change due to the decrease of alcohol in the land. In certain parishes the use of ardent spirits was almost entirely absent. Many pub owners abandoned their trade due to lack of sales and also as a result of new holy convictions. Some professed that drunkenness had been annihilated. Although this was too great a claim, the influence of alcohol had been broken in the land in an amazing and miraculous way.

One of the preachers greatly used at this time was Henry Grattan Guinness (1835–1910), grandson of Arthur Guinness, who founded the famous Irish brewery. Henry's father Capt. John Guinness (1783–1850) was converted late in life through the Wesleyan Methodists, and as the first teetotaller in the family and abstainer from all alcohol he withdrew from his partnership in the brewery.

Young Henry Grattan, along with C.H. Spurgeon and D.L. Moody, was considered one of the greatest preachers of that generation. He spent a year ceaselessly preaching all over England, Scotland, Wales, and across Europe, before preaching to great crowds in Dublin city in January 1858. In March of that same year he preached three times a day to great crowds in Belfast, including ministers and students in training for the ministry. He left Ireland at the end of that year, but returned in 1859 to preach in the midst of the full flow of revival to crowds of 20,000 people in the open air. His strong stance on abstinence left a profound mark upon Ulster right down to recent times. In the following decades he became the primary catalyst of an astounding worldwide missionary effort.

During the mid and late 19th Century, the churches in England and North America were constantly impacted by local and national revivals during which such diverse vessels as D.L.

Moody, William Booth, F.B. Meyer, Charles Finney, A.B. Simpson, and a host of others, were used to gather in a great harvest of souls. Each of these men practised and taught total abstinence. Little wonder then that Catherine Booth reported that by the end of the 19th Century, almost all protestant ministers in North America were total abstainers

Even stalwart occasional drinkers, like C.H. Spurgeon, were eventually won over to the temperance cause in his latter days. Politicians and royalty looked on with joy and stood guard over the temperance cause, both in the Church and in secular society. Queen Victoria was the president of the temperance movement in England, which she supported wholeheartedly.

These continual waves of revival which intermittently broke upon the church, beginning in the 16th Century, dealt a death blow to social drinking and restored the truth of total abstinence to the church. This reached its climax at the end of the 19th and beginning of the 20th Centuries, as various new *Holiness* and *Deeper Life* movements carried the Gospel to many other nations with missionary zeal.

Into the new century, the Pentecostal movement taught this truth and it spread quickly and widely across many nations and diverse cultures. The biggest Pentecostal denomination in the world today is the Assemblies of God (AoG). The American AoG set forth a very clear statement in an official paper in 1985 maintaining the strong stance on total abstinence which was held by its founders.

The list could go on as we recount how abstinence was restored to the Church in many other nations, by other great preachers, spiritual movements and mighty revivals which changed the face of society, and frequently saved it from utter destruction, but this is merely an overview drawn from 500 years of spiritual movements and genuine revivals.

Needless to say, at times of declension, compromise and apostasy, social drinking and drunkenness prosper in the world as well as in the midst of what is called the Church. With the rise of intellectualism, the influence of the world, programmes and strategies of men the simple truths of Scripture get obscured, hidden and buried until the Spirit of the Lord reveals them again to chosen vessels who will believe them, live them, preach them and teach them to a people who will receive them.

I am fully persuaded that in the next Holy Ghost revival, this issue shall be dealt with in the hearts of those who make up the true Church of Jesus Christ. Once again our nations are being severely damaged by addiction to alcohol. The crime rate, destruction to family and home life, and the terrible effects in the church are increasing and getting out of hand. Only a gracious spiritual revival will stem this terrible tide and restore to God's people this wonderful truth of total abstinence from alcohol.

CHAPTER 10
LEGALISM OR LIBERTY?

The two great weapons social drinkers have used against abstainers are firstly, the ancient art of **name-calling** and secondly, taking certain texts of Scripture utterly out of their context by misinterpreting them.

With the first of these, they have gained much ground by calling abstainers, *legalists*. To be thought legalistic in this generation is worse than having leprosy in the ancient world. To make a person or doctrine unclean and untouchable through name-calling is a very cunning trick.

With the second they have supported their name-calling by 'high-jacking' certain scriptures and promoting their own personal interpretation of them so strongly, repeatedly and widely that people now think this is what the Bible actually says.

By this means they have laid an almost immovable foundation for this stronghold of social drinking which has gained much ground amongst Evangelicals in this generation. *But our weapons are not carnal* and we do not and must not stoop to use either of these weapons. We must use the artillery of God's unchanging Truth by comparing scripture with scripture and so bring this stronghold tumbling down by breaking up its foundation by the power of God's truth alone.

Andre S. Bustanoby, in his book *The wrath of grapes: Drinking and the Church Divided,* takes the effectual ancient weapon of name-calling as his foremost means of attack against those who believe in abstinence. In his first two chapters, covering 19 pages, he directly uses the words *legalist, legalistic* and *legalism* at least 73 times and infers legalism in many other instances. His primary definition of a legalist is an abstainer from alcohol who believes others should abstain.

He also has to admit that a *legalist* is someone who establishes teachings which are not in the Bible and who then makes everyone else conform to them. But by this second accurate definition, the abstainer is most certainly not a *legalist*—on the contrary, the abstainer is a lover of Jesus Christ who keeps the written Word hidden in his heart and who has no desire to grieve the Holy Ghost by drinking alcohol.

G.I. Williamson used the same weapon when he wrote his book *Wine in the Bible*. In reference to the teaching held in I Timothy 4 he states: "those who desire to impose a law of total abstinence upon Christians are departing from the truth of God and following the doctrine of demons. It is demonic to locate evil in any material thing."[18] Again referring to the same text he states: "...there is no greater need in the church today than to reject this doctrine of devils." He also speaks of the "false doctrine of mandatory total abstinence."[19]

Then most recently Jim West, in his book *Drinking with Calvin and Luther,* used these weapons again in referring to I Timothy 4:3. He states: "the Bible teaches that wine is food; if we despise it, then we have unwittingly placed ourselves in the camp of those who have departed from the faith during the latter days."[20] In the last chapter of his book he offers a new, contemporary pledge for those to sign who have been converted to social-drinking. Just one line states: "I acknowledge my sin and my uninstructed conscience, as well as my pharisaic attitude towards those who drink wine and beer to the glory of God."[21]

As you can see these two weapons are put to good use in the writings of the social-drinking camp. It saddens me to have to add a chapter like this but false accusation must be met head-

---

[18] p.14, *Wine in the Bible,* G.I. Williamson
[19] p. 44 Ibid
[20] p.25-26, *Drinking with Calvin and Luther,* Jim West
[21] p. 178 Ibid

on with truth. This false accusation of legalism must be unmasked. It is a very serious thing to accuse genuine sincere believers of false doctrine, of holding to doctrines of demons and of departing from the faith purely because they are convinced that the Bible teaches total abstinence from alcohol.

Let us look at I Timothy 4, and see exactly what the apostle Paul was saying. *"Now the Spirit speaketh expressly, that in the latter times some shall depart from the faith, giving heed to seducing spirits, and doctrines of devils; Speaking lies in hypocrisy; having their conscience seared with a hot iron; Forbidding to marry, and commanding to abstain from meats, which God hath created to be received with thanksgiving of them which believe and know the truth. For every creature of God is good, and nothing to be refused, if it be received with thanksgiving: For it is sanctified by the word of God and prayer."*

Please note, that this scripture is dealing with foods not drinks. Alcohol is not only a drink but a drink that is elsewhere warned against, condemned and forbidden. This scripture is certainly not encouraging believers to eat harmful and poisonous foods neither is it encouraging believers to drink alcohol as a part of their Christian faith to prove that they are orthodox in the faith. Also, the abstainer is not one who is speaking lies, neither is his conscience seared. In fact he is speaking the written truth and his conscience is very alive and sensitive on this issue.

To try and infer that abstainers have departed from the faith as a part of the end day apostasy is a shocking accusation. This is in itself an infringement on the conscience, liberty, rights and Christian freedom of born-again believers who abstain from alcohol. It is also religious manipulation and intimidation of the worst kind. To call someone a *legalist* repeatedly in order to get them to yield is playground bullying.

The true believer does not use such tactics and weapons. He lays out truth convincingly in order to win his brother or sister over to a better and more perfect way. To place someone outside Christ, salvation and truth on the basis of their conviction on alcohol is more serious than we can possibly imagine. These authors are reckless in taking I Timothy 4 utterly out of context and judging abstainers by their new interpretation.

If the doctrine of social drinking is true then let them confront us with Scripture set in its right context instead of foolish accusations. To use these tactics instead of sincere persuasion only reveals the weakness of their arguments. However, I do appreciate that there are those like Gentry in the social drinking camp who have not used the weapons of name-calling and mockery when writing on this subject.

Let us look at a few other scriptures which are used out of context and repeatedly to uphold this stronghold of social drinking and also let us take a close, honest and sincere look to see if abstainers are guilty in any way of legalism.

Should We Judge Those Who Drink?

In Colossians chapter two, it would seem that Paul is telling us to judge no man according to what he eats or drinks. He says, *"Let no man therefore judge you in meat, or in drink, or in respect of an holyday, or of the new moon, or of the sabbath days: Which are a shadow of things to come; but the body is of Christ"* (Col.2:16-17).

Social-drinkers have often used this verse against anyone who would disagree with them or who would judge them for drinking alcohol. They teach that this verse concerning *"drink"* includes alcohol and so they feel perfectly justified in walking free from any guilt or condemnation that could be caused by anyone raising questions about their drinking habits. By this means they ease their conscience from any concern and free themselves from any conviction of sin in relation to their use of alcohol.

However in this passage we must understand that Paul is talking about religious festivals as taught under the Old Testament law which were all a shadow of things to come. The Old Testament shadow gave way to the New Testament reality brought in by Christ and manifested in the Church which is His body.

In fact it is almost an exact quote from Ezekiel 45:17, *"And it shall be the prince's part to give burnt offerings, and meat offerings, and drink offerings, in the feasts, and in the new moons, and in the sabbaths, in all solemnities of the house of Israel:"*

The *"drink"* Paul is talking about is the drink offering used in the Jewish feasts. This has nothing to do with the issue of socially drinking alcohol but rather the rejection of Levitical ceremonial drink offerings, which were only a shadow, pointing to Christ. Paul says that this *"handwriting of ordinances"* had been blotted out through *"nailing it to his cross"* (v14).

The drink offering was *"a shadow of things to come"* and was fulfilled in the sacrifice of Jesus Christ at Calvary. But no Old Testament warning or command concerning alcohol has been disannulled at the Cross.

Paul was telling the Christians at Colossae that they were not to come under pressure from the Jewish Christians to conform to the Jewish rituals. He was telling them to not let these Jewish Christians judge them in relation to the drink offering. When he said, *"Let no man therefore judge you...in drink"*, he was instructing this church to not allow these Judaizers to make condemning damning decisions about their walk in Christ on the basis of Jewish drink offerings. They were free from such judgements.

A little further on, Paul says if you *"are dead with Christ"*, then you are not subject to such *"ordinances"* as *"Touch not; taste not; handle not."* Again the social drinker uses this text to proclaim his freedom, liberty and right to drink alcohol. He believes that when someone tells him to "not drink" then this scripture applies. But Paul writes this in relation to *"the commandments and doctrines of men."* This teaching of *"taste not"* was in reference to man-made teachings which Paul says the church at Colossae ought to resist and from which they ought to walk free.

This was a realm of teaching distinct from the Jewish law which the Colossians had to resist. These teachings of *"Touch not; taste not; handle not"* were not Old Testament teachings but things which were being added by men. For this very reason they were to be rejected.

This is a far cry from the practice of social drinkers who use these verses to proclaim that they are free from all guilt and condemnation caused by those who say "taste not." This is yet another example of how some social drinkers take scripture totally out of context in order to justify the social drinking of alcohol.

While they accuse the abstainer of taking scripture out of context and of walking in 'legalism' they are in fact the ones who are taking scripture out of context and who are walking in 'license'—which is the action of walking free from the clear commands and teachings contained in the Bible.

Christian Liberty, Legalism & License

A vital issue connected to the whole discussion on alcohol and the Christian is Christian liberty. By liberty is meant the right and freedom of a Christian, who is in Christ under Grace, to participate in what does not contradict the written Scriptures and to be free from all man-made teachings, practices and pressure.

Social drinkers take the teaching contained in Romans 14 and raise their banner over it, and build their arguments upon it in order to try and prove that the Christian who drinks alcohol does so as a part of their freedom and liberty in Christ. Therefore any attack upon their right to drink alcohol is considered an attack on the very foundation of their Christian liberty.

Romans 14, deals with the contention between *"weak"* and *"strong"* believers in the church at Rome. One of the issues of contention is that the strong *"believeth that he may eat all things"* but the weak only eats *"herbs."* Paul's instruction is that the strong Christian is not to *"despise"* or to think little of this weak believer and his opinions. The weak believer is also instructed to not *"judge"* the strong one who feels at liberty according to God's Word to *"eat all things."*

Both of them have the freedom to either eat, or not eat, according to their own conscience. There is nothing essentially sinful about only eating herbs, and there is nothing essentially sinful in eating all things including meat.

Scripture is clear that both *"meats"* and *"herbs"* have been given for man to eat (Gen.1:29-30; 9:3; I Tim.4:4). Because of this the herb-eater (vegetarian) is called *"weak"* because he is abstaining for conscience sake from something God allows. This 'weak' man expects others to do likewise, but Paul is saying, that whilst the 'weak' has liberty to abstain, he should not judge anyone else for eating all foods, including meat, for meat is clearly permitted by God and commended in the Scriptures; both in the Old and New Testament.

Paul goes further in his first letter to Timothy when he writes that in the last days *"some shall depart from the faith, giving heed to seducing spirits, and doctrines of devils."* Amongst these teachers will be those *"commanding to abstain from meats, which God hath created to be received with thanksgiving..."* (4:1-3). Please note, that these teachers command something that is not commanded by God in the Scriptures.

Of course all such doctrines are to be resisted when forced or compelled upon true believers. **This is true Christian liberty. It is a liberty to walk in the light of God's Word without adding to it or taking from it.**

The Bible is clear in its teaching in the New Testament that eating habits do not make one more or less spiritual, (unless gluttony is involved) and so we are not to judge people according to manmade opinions concerning foods (I Cor.8:8; Heb.13:9).

Paul goes further in chapter 14 to deal with those who *"esteem one day above another"* as opposed to those who *"esteem every day alike."* He says: *"Let every man be fully persuaded in his own mind"* (v5). This was concerning special feast days and fasts; certain dates set aside as sacred unto God. This is not concerning the Lord's Day. He is not saying make your own decision concerning the weekly gathering of believers to remember Christ's death. He is talking about numbers of Jewish or secular feast days.

It is at this point that the social drinker raises the issue of alcohol. In Romans 14, the drinking of wine is not explicitly dealt with but is presumed from verse 17 which says: *"For the kingdom of God is not meat and drink; but righteousness, and peace, and joy in the Holy Ghost."* Then in verse 21 wine drinking is clearly mentioned in relation to the *"weak"* believer: *"It is good neither to eat flesh, nor to drink wine, nor any thing whereby thy brother stumbleth, or is offended, or is made weak."*

In response to this we must first point out that verse 21 is not talking about alcoholic wine. It is talking about a drink that is allowed for the strong believer. It is talking about the fruit of the wine, grape juice—unfermented wine. We have already seen that alcohol is condemned in the rest of Scripture and in other writings by Paul. Paul would not contradict himself by allowing fermented wine here while condemning it elsewhere.

In this chapter the weak believer is abstaining from things which by God he is allowed to take. We know that unfermented wine is most certainly allowed by God and that the weak believer should not judge the strong believer if he drinks such an innocent drink.

Before, during and after the First Century, there were various movements within Judaism and Christianity which abstained from drinking the pure, unfermented juice of the grape. John the Baptist and some of those who followed him held to this custom, as did James the Lord's brother, and young Timothy. The weak believer at Rome took this practice and made it a binding law upon all. His weak conscience caused him to turn an 'allowance' into a 'law' which then became more of a snare to him than an aid to holiness.

But Paul says if the drinking of wine which *is* allowed is going to be a means of this delicate believer tripping up, becoming weak in his walk and even falling into sin, then it is best to abstain from such wine. This is not dealing with someone who disagrees with drinking alcohol but someone very weak who could fall away from the faith through strong Christians insisting on drinking grape juice or eating flesh.

This does not mean that the strong Christian who is walking according to the written Scriptures must abstain from grape juice for the rest of his life any more than it means he must forsake eating meat for the rest of his life for the sake of the Vegetarian. This is talking about certain specific occasions when temporary abstinence from meat or wine (grape juice) will be right in order to not cause a great grieving of a weak believer's conscience.

This is not talking about the typical situation with the average believer but about an unusually weak believer who just cannot grasp the simplicity of freedom in Christ or the clear teaching of Scripture concerning these things. It is an extreme case; an unusual case.

These verses are not dealing with a difference of opinion or conviction over alcohol but of the serious danger of a weak Christian stumbling in their walk because a strong Christian demands his liberty to exercise his right and freedom to drink the fruit of the vine.

It is sad to say that in this day not only do those who think themselves strong in their walk insist on drinking innocent grape juice but they also insist on drinking alcohol without hindrance and go on to look down upon any who abstain, regarding them legalistic. They even go much further by pressing young weak believers against their own conscience and amidst serious and sincere concerns to exercise their so-called liberty and to prove their freedom in Christ by drinking alcohol.

Abstainers have also frequently misunderstood this chapter. They often use it to set forth an argument that if wine-drinking is likely to cause a genuine but weak believer to stumble into sin or to be tempted, then the stronger believer should totally abstain from alcohol.

While this sounds very good and righteous, this chapter actually does not teach total abstinence from alcoholic wine for the sake of weak believers. It teaches a temporary abstinence on certain occasions from unfermented grape juice for the sake of a weak believer.

It is abstinence from a thing which is elsewhere allowed in Scripture for all believers but from which the weak believer, through ignorance, abstains and expects all believers to do likewise.

As we have already seen, alcohol is condemned in all of Scripture, both Old and New Testament, under law and under Grace. Therefore it is not appropriate to place it in Romans 14 as 'neutral', nor is it appropriate to apply what Paul teaches in Romans 14 to alcohol. To do so would be to ignore the rest of Scripture and to make this one chapter override the rest of Scripture—to contradict what Paul teaches elsewhere.

When the social drinker makes his stand for liberty based on this chapter, he is making a grave mistake. That he would think that he has the freedom and right to drink alcohol according to his own conscience is not according to God's Word. There is no such freedom or right.

A Christian's conscience is not totally free to do as he pleases for he is bound by God Himself through His written Word. The conscience is never free to disobey the teaching and instruction of Scripture. This theory concerning Christian liberty in drinking alcohol can only be supported if it can be shown clearly that alcohol is lawful, biblical, allowed, commanded and promoted elsewhere in Scripture. But as we have seen this is not so; in fact quite the opposite.

Of course many through wrong teaching or lack of instruction make genuine mistakes in these things. While we fully understand that they may be sincerely wrong that does not excuse them. We must endeavour to graciously, carefully and biblically enlighten such believers to the truth.

Paul teaches in this chapter that even allowable things are forsaken out of a desire to edify others, to prefer others and in considering others. How much more should someone not be willing to then forsake alcohol for the good of others? To claim Christian liberty while drinking the poison of Sodom is a perversion of biblical liberty and a denial of the true freedom of conscience.

Someone who is dependent on alcohol as a normal regular drink or who frequently crosses the safe line of sobriety is hardly experiencing true Christian freedom and liberty. While he speaks of his right and liberty to drink, in reality he has become a prisoner and slave to a habit and a substance that has destroyed great multitudes in every nation and in every generation. Even great and godly men like Noah have been struck down in one moment of time by this deadly substance yet Christians think they can proclaim Christian liberty by playing with this dangerous fire.

There are other scriptures which social drinkers take out of context but I hope this is sufficient to deal with this much abused and ridiculous use of liberty and so-called freedom of the conscience. It is an abuse of Grace when liberty is used for licence in tolerating what the Scriptures condemn.

CHAPTER 11
QUESTIONS AND ANSWERS

In answering genuine questions we must remember that there are honest inquirers who need sound, biblical answers set in their correct context. It is regrettable that a number of abstainers have often not been able to give the clear biblical response required for such inquirers, or at times abstainers have satisfied their conscience and have been content to say that they know from the Holy Spirit that drinking is wrong, or that in their own heart they know that abstinence is right.

While I agree with their stance on abstinence, such responses are not sufficient for those who have been incorrectly taught or who are genuinely seeking for guidance on the subject of alcohol and the Bible. Such abstainers are no different from the social drinker who says that he feels 'ok' in his heart before God about drinking alcohol; or the social drinker who says that the Holy Spirit lets him know when to stop drinking.

Such responses from both sides are not acceptable or satisfactory. We must know and understand what the written Scriptures say. We must then make these written truths our only answer. Believers on both sides of this argument are wrong if they follow a vague, mystical guidance, personal opinion, or even a personal conviction. **It is time to be fully convinced and persuaded by the written Word of God.**

As we near the end of this book, I also want to warn abstainers about being puffed up with knowledge. We must be careful of pride in 'having the answers'. We must hold truth carefully and humbly. **I believe that there are social drinkers whose knowledge is wrong but their hearts are pure. I also believe that there are abstainers whose knowledge is correct but their hearts are wrong.**

Paul, the apostle, wisely says: *"Now as touching things offered unto idols, we know that we all have knowledge. Knowledge puffeth up, but charity edifieth"* (I Cor.8:1).

When the truth about social drinking is understood and united with sincere love in the heart, it will edify true believers rather than leading to mocking or name-calling. Anyone can state truth, but not everyone has the maturity to win someone over by persuasion from the Scriptures. A parrot can repeat statements but it takes a sincere, prayerful, humble Christian to minister the truth as it is in Christ Jesus.

We have already dealt with many questions, problems, controversies and fables in the previous chapters but this present chapter allows us to summarise some and go more in-depth in others.

I would simply warn you however that if you do not allow this book to drive you into the written Word where you can be fully taught, established and anchored in God's truth, then someone else will argue you out of abstinence from alcohol. Please allow the Spirit of God to teach you correctly, biblically and permanently.

Questions Concerning the Old Testament

Q. In Genesis 43:34 we read concerning Joseph entertaining his brethren: *"And they drank, and were merry with him."* The term *"merry"* which is used here is the Hebrew word *shakar*. This is the word from which we get our word *"strong drink" (shekar)*. It means to drink abundantly, to drink until you're fully satisfied or to become intoxicated. When used of Noah it certainly meant intoxication *(Gen.9:21)*. When Eli accused Hannah of being drunk with wine it was the same *(I Sam.1:14)*, and when David made Uriah drunk it again meant intoxication *(II Sam.11:13)*.

When we study the 19 places where it is used in the Old Testament it is very easy to see that it always relates to the drinking of fermented wine and alcohol which either makes you happy or drunk (Isa.29:9; Hab.2:15 etc). Of course I do not believe in drinking to the point of drunkenness but surely this must reveal that to become merry, happy, relaxed or joyful through wine has the support and blessing of God?

A. You are correct in saying that this word ***shakar*** **means to drink abundantly** or **drink until you're full or satisfied**. If you *shakar* (drink), an alcoholic drink you will be intoxicated but if you *shakar* a drink that is not fermented, then you most certainly will not be intoxicated but simply full or satisfied. **Each time the word *shakar* is used whether you become drunk or satisfied depends upon whether the drink is fermented or not.**

Let me show you two different scriptures where *shakar* is used yet cannot and does not mean drunkenness but only satisfaction. The first of these is in the context of wine (*yayin*).

"I have drunk my wine [yayin] *with my milk: eat, O friends; drink, yea, drink abundantly* [shakar], *O beloved."* (Song.5:1). Solomon here writes a wonderful pure love song about the Shepherd and the Shulamite as a type of Christ and the Church. Here is a call for the Shulamite to drink wine, *yayin*, abundantly, or to the point of *shakar*. It was a call for her to drink wine to a **point of full satisfaction.** If this wine had been fermented this would have been a sin; but if it was the fresh, unfermented juice of the grape this would be a very safe instruction.

As a matter of fact, the nature of alcohol is that it may initially lift the drinker's mood, but this is a very temporary state and therefore very **unsatisfying.** The nature of Alcohol is that the drinker is NEVER satisfied and one drink leads to another, which leads to another, which is the very opposite of satisfaction. Alcohol cannot *shakar*.

Furthermore, are we to imagine that Solomon would promote such an instruction between two lovers in this, the greatest love story ever told? This is the same Solomon who said that we are not to look upon wine when it was fermented; that intoxicating drinks are like poison; that such drinks were mockers in character and that kings and princes were not to drink it under any condition.

Also we read in this verse of the practice of those days of mixing unfermented wine with milk or honey. This is spoken of in Proverbs 9:1-2, by Solomon: *"Wisdom hath...mingled her wine."* An intoxicating drink was not mixed with milk and honey.

Some popular contemporary preachers have not only misinterpreted the whole book of the Song of Solomon, but with it have taken this scripture out of context, making it the basis of teaching that a husband and wife may enjoy each other through the intoxicating influence of alcoholic wine.

Secondly, in Haggai 1:6, *shekar* again means to drink until the point of satisfaction: *"ye eat, but ye have not enough; ye drink, but ye are not filled with drink* [shekar]; *ye clothe you, but there is none warm."* This is not talking about drunkenness but satisfaction.

These scriptures reveal that *shakar* can be used in an innocent healthy way to mean that someone drinks to the point of satisfaction but also of someone drinking to the point of intoxication. It depends on the type of drink and the context.

Q. *But that still does not explain how Joseph and his brethren could be "merry" through drinking grape juice (Gen.43:34). We read in Ps.104:15 of "wine that maketh glad the heart of man"; in Esther 1:10 that "the heart of the king was merry with wine"; in I Samuel 25:36 that "Nabal's heart was merry within him, for he was very drunken"; in II Samuel 13:28 that "Amnon's heart is merry with wine"; in Ecclesiastes 9:7 "Go thy way, eat thy bread with joy, and drink thy wine with a merry heart; for God now accepteth thy works, and finally in Zechariah 10:7 that "their heart shall rejoice as through wine." You just cannot get away from it: wine was created by God to bring joy, happiness and gladness. How can you possibly deny this?*

A. As with *shakar* **context is crucial**. When it speaks of King Ahasuerus, Nabal, and Amnon in the above scriptures it reveals that they were all *merry* through wine that was intoxicating. When it says *merry* it is speaking of that temporary and even deceptive mirth that comes to the heart through alcohol. Please note, however, that when it says that these three men were *merry*, it is not commended in any of these three accounts and little good came of it.

One made an unwise request of his wife; one was drunk when David was on his way to kill him and the last was killed during his drunken stupor. The warning is proved to be correct: **deceit is contained in fermented drinks**. Of course there is a frivolity, joy, rejoicing or happiness that comes with it but it is a falsely created, **temporary mood** and emotion. How sad that some think that the Lord promotes this. Solomon was clear in recommending this only for those in a very desperate state (Prov.31:6).

Intoxication is a state well known to God's people throughout each era of Bible history. None of God's people has ever been ignorant of it but mentioning it does not equate to condoning it. We may hear the abstainer mention intoxication or use it as an example, but it does not mean that he condones it or commends it.

This is what is done in Zechariah 9:15, and again in 10:7. The 'noise' and 'rejoicing' of a drunkard is used as an example. It uses the important word *"as."* Again, this is not commending the state of drunkenness at all.

When someone tries to justify the social drinking doctrine they must go a step further and justify the effects of being *merry*. That is why Kenneth L. Gentry, in his book *God Gave Wine*, which promotes social drinking, says: "the 'gladdening effect' of wine is acceptable, at least to some degree (Ps.104:15; Ecc.9:7; 10:19; II Sam.13:28; Est.1:10; Zech.9:15; 10:7; Jdg.9:13)"[22] And again when speaking of Psalm 104: "in fact, a moderate 'gladdening of the heart' is not forbidden, according to this and other scriptures."[23]

So those who promote social drinking must justify this state of mirth which is created by alcohol. In reality it is impossible to drink an intoxicating drink without being affected in some degree, even if undetected. But it is also the witness of those who habitually drink alcohol moderately, that they

---
[22] p.96 *God Gave Wine*, Kenneth L. Gentry
[23] p.53 ibid

periodically stray over their own set line of sobriety and begin to feel the effects of the alcohol upon mind, mouth and movement. Sadly, this is justified—with confidence—on the basis of the above scriptures.

Joseph and his brethren were either *merry* through intoxication or merry through being fully satisfied with what they drank and by the kind reception given by Joseph. When it says that they *"drank"* the word *shathah* is used which means to imbibe, to drink deeply or fully. It is used frequently throughout the Old Testament and many times in relation to drinking water. In this passage it does not state explicitly what they drank. If Joseph and his brethren were intoxicated then the merriness which resulted is utterly condemned elsewhere in Scripture. There is no justification for becoming merry through being full of fermented wine.

But this is highly unlikely when we consider the context. At this point Joseph had not revealed himself to his brothers. Would he now drop his guard by becoming merry through intoxication?

To assume that it always means moderate intoxication when the word *merry* is mentioned is going too far. It is strange indeed to insinuate that only intoxicating wine can bring joy to the heart. From all of this we see that at times it is clear that it means the intoxicating influence of wine, but at other times it definitely does not.

As we have previously seen when dealing with *tirosh* (the grape harvest), it never means intoxicating wine and very rarely grape juice yet we are told that it *"cheereth"* and *"gladdens"* the heart. *"And the vine said unto them, Should I leave my wine* [tirosh], *which cheereth God and man, and go to be promoted over the trees?"* (Jdg.9:13). And again: *"Thou hast put gladness in my heart, more than in the time that their corn and their wine* [tirosh] *increase"* (Ps.4:7). These scriptures are not talking about the effect of intoxicating wine but the joy concerning bringing in the harvest.

Q. *In Deuteronomy 14:26, Moses instructs the people: "And thou shalt bestow that money for whatsoever thy soul lusteth after, for oxen, or for sheep, or for wine, or for strong drink, or for whatsoever thy soul desireth: and thou shalt eat there before the LORD thy God, and thou shalt rejoice, thou, and thine household."* Here is a clear command for Israel to purchase whatsoever their soul *"lusteth after"* ('avah) as well as *"desireth"* (sha'al). The first word means to covet, desire or long after; the second means to require, request or demand. This desire for wine (yayin) and strong drink (shekar) is clearly allowed, promoted and encouraged. This was to be a part of a feast in the presence of God by whole families. I believe this reveals the clear blessing of God upon these drinks in a religious setting for the enjoyment of God's people. I believe this is unanswerable by those who abstain from alcohol and who desire or pressure others to abstain. What is your response?

A. In the previous verses to the one that you mention we read of the normal standard practice of all Israel: this was to be the tithe of all the harvest from every seed and the harvests of the field—corn, wine and oil (14:22-23). In verse 23, it says that they brought *"wine"* (*tirosh*) which as we saw in chapter two was the actual grape harvest from which fresh juice was extracted, which without question was unfermented. So this was the normal practice for this celebration.

Please also note that nowhere in these verses does it mention drinking, it only talks of eating before the Lord (v23, 26). Of course one could argue that drinking was included, as no doubt it was, but no mention is actually made concerning drinking strong drink (*shekar*). These verses most certainly are not revealing that we as God's people can drink alcohol. It does however reveal that the standard practice for all the families of Israel was to *"eat...wine"* (*tirosh*) at the feast. Prior to these verses we have many instructions about eating clean and unclean food (v3-21).

The scripture you mention was not the normal standard practice for all Israel but the exception to the rule. In verse 24-26 we see that *"if"* the feast and celebration was too far from where they lived they could turn their tithes into money and upon reaching the feast they could purchase all the products mentioned in the verse you quote.

But why, you may ask, does the normal practice of bringing *"wine"* (*tirosh*) now become the exception to the rule of buying *"wine"* (*yayin*) and *"strong drink"* (*shekar*)? Why is the wonderful fruit of the grape harvest now exchanged for wine and strong drink which were fermented and introduced into this feast in this singular exception?

The answer is simple. In Numbers 28:7 we are told: *"And **the drink offering** thereof shall be the fourth part of an hin for the one lamb: in the holy place shalt thou cause the strong wine (shekar) to be **poured** unto the LORD for a drink offering."* The drink offering was not drunk but **poured out.** This took place in the holy place in the presence of God during the feast. Strong drink or as it is translated here, *"strong wine"* (*shekar*), was brought to the feast for this one specific purpose. We also read elsewhere that *"wine"* (*yayin*), was also used in the drink offering and poured out before the Lord (Ex.29:40). This again explains why wine (*yayin*) which was fermented was purchased for the feast.

The drinking of strong drink (*shekar*) is condemned throughout the Old Testament. To make this verse mean the drinking of *shekar* by God's people would contradict other scriptures; but understanding it as I have explained contradicts no other scripture. There is no reason at all to infer or think that this could have been a fermented drink which Israel drank at the feast. This feast was a call to holiness and was a demonstration of fearing God as they obeyed all of Scripture in the very presence of the Lord.

Q. *In the Old Testament the priests were told that they were not to drink wine or strong drink when ministering to God in the Temple. Does this mean that we as New Testament believers/priests should not drink when attending church gatherings but are allowed to drink when at home or on holiday?*

A. It most certainly does not. If it is wrong in church then it is still wrong at home. If we take this Old Testament type and bring it over to the New Testament believer we see that we, born-again believers, are now the temple of the Holy Spirit. We are told in I Cor.3:16: *"Know ye not that ye are the temple of God, and that* *the Spirit of God dwelleth in you?"* And again in 6:19: *"What? know ye not that your body is the temple of the Holy Ghost which is in you, which ye have of God, and ye are not your own?"*

In the Old Testament no alcoholic influence was allowed in the temple. This is now carried over into the New Testament in a spiritual manner and applied to the physical body of a believer. Paul gives a serious warning to those who disregard this fact *"If any man defile the temple of God, him shall God destroy; for the temple of God is holy, which temple ye are"* (3:17).

The standard for the New Testament believer filled with the Spirit of God cannot be less than the standard maintained in the Old Testament temple building. We have been redeemed by the precious blood and are indwelt by Christ through the Holy Spirit. We must not defile God's temple with intoxicating drink.

But more than that, just because the Old Testament priesthood was forbidden to drink such beverages when they entered the temple does not mean that it was allowed when not in the temple. As we have seen in previous chapters strong drink and intoxicating drinks were never allowed—not at any time.

Q. *I have often read and heard that the **water supply** in ancient Israel was contaminated so wine was drunk instead or it was mixed with the water to sterilize it. Surely this proves that the wine of the Bible had to be fermented or else it would not have sterilized the water?*

A. This is yet another inaccurate claim because firstly the water supply *was* mostly fine in Israel. A precious resource to this land which can often experience drought, the supply and protection of water, has always been a top priority to Israel—ancient and modern. In Jerusalem, archaeological evidence shows that particular care and effort was made to specifically protect the water supply to the city, which came forth from the precious Gihon Spring outside of the city. The engineering of reservoirs and water supply channels pioneered by this great nation was very sophisticated.

Throughout the Bible, we have frequent references to the drinking of water. From what we read in both New and Old Testaments, we know that water was only scarce in a drought, a siege or for some other reason such as the incident at Jericho, (I Sam.9:11; 30:11 etc). Bread and water are mentioned together numbers of times throughout the scriptures as the two basic necessities of life (I Kgs.18:4 etc). A man can manage without wine but not without water.

Furthermore, I challenge you to research just how much alcohol (percentage) is necessary to effectively sterilize drinking water.

Questions Concerning the New Testament

Q. *I want to ask about* **Jesus turning the water into wine** *at the marriage feast at Cana of Galilee in John 2:1-11. It seems that according to the custom of the day it was normal for a marriage ceremony and celebration to last for a week. In these Scriptures we read that when He came to the wedding His mother Mary informed Him that there was no more wine and showed every sign of encouraging Him to do something to provide wine for the guests. We are then told that after Jesus turned the water into wine, the servants took it to the governor of the feast who tasted it and then said to the bridegroom: "Every man at the beginning doth set forth good wine; and when men have well drunk, then that which is worse: but thou hast kept the good wine until now" (John 2:10).*

The term used here "...when men have well drunk..." is the Greek word 'methuo' which means to drink to the point of intoxication, to get drunk or be drunk. The seven times this word is used in the New Testament it means a state of intoxication as a result of drinking alcohol. Surely the governor here means that the tradition at weddings was to wait until people were happy, tipsy or drunk as a result of drinking the wine and then to serve a poor quality wine whereas in this particular case this tradition was broken by Jesus serving better wine than what the guests had already drunk?

A. Let's look at what this would mean if you are correct. It would mean that Jesus not only encouraged the social drinking of alcohol at such times, but also encouraged and aided drunken parties. If this is so, then Jesus was here contradicting other statements that He made elsewhere about the sin and danger of drunkenness. Also He would be contradicting the clear teaching of Solomon's wisdom, who said, 'Don't even look at wine when it is fermented.' He would also be contradicting the strong warnings of the prophets against such practices and of the apostles who taught against such a practice.

This is a very serious accusation against Christ. Straight after this we are told in verses 14-17, that Jesus was eaten up with zeal for His Father's House when seeing that religion had become merchandise in the Temple. He made a whip and chased the sellers out of the Temple. Would the Son of God go from promoting drunkenness in Cana to punishing covetousness in the Temple? No, not at all; it would constitute a contradiction.

Furthermore, the governor at the wedding did not say that the people at this wedding were *"drunk."* He was saying that it was the custom of many at such occasions to be *methuo*. This word can also mean when men have 'well drunk' or '**drunk to the full**.' That is why Wycliffe, Coverdale and many other translators of the English Bible, who were fluent in Greek and Hebrew, translated it with these words which were clearer and more explicit.

I do not at all believe that Jesus produced alcoholic wine or encouraged drunkenness. He made new wine which carried no element of alcohol.

Also the bridegroom had obviously invited Mary, Jesus and His disciples because he was in sympathy with this new prophet of righteousness. No doubt, it was a godly upright wedding celebration with no reproach involved. Later on in this same book we read of *"Nathanael of Cana in Galilee"* who was one of Christ's twelve disciples (21:2). As it happens Nathanael became a follower of Christ just prior to this wedding feast and may have been the means of Christ's invitation (1:45-51). **(Please note that Chapter 12, *Christ, Wine and Alcohol*, also deals with this scripture.)**

Q. *But does it not also say in I Cor.11:21 in reference to the church at Corinth who gathered to partake of the Lord's Supper, that: "For in eating every one taketh before other his own supper: and one is hungry, and another is drunken." Here we* have a clear statement saying that there were those who were drunk at the Lord's Table. Does this not show that alcoholic wine was drunk at Church gatherings and for communion in the Corinthian church?

A. In this chapter particularly we see the practice of the *agape meal* or love feast which was common in the early Church. When they gathered together to eat they would bring their own food to the supper then break bread together in remembrance of the Lord's death. In this particular verse the context is *"eating...supper."* Resulting from this came two problems. Firstly, some did not have much or bring much with them, and so remained hungry at the meal. Secondly, others were *"drunk"*, or as the word correctly means, they were 'fully satisfied' after eating their plenteous meal. This makes full sense then, 'one was hungry and the other was full.' Paul uses the word *"hungry"* as the opposite of being *"drunk."* If he had meant to say that the person was intoxicated he would have contrasted him with a sober man, not a hungry man.

What is Paul's response to all this? In the following verse he says *"What? have ye not houses to eat and to drink in?"* and then later in v33-34, *"Wherefore, my brethren, when ye come together to eat, tarry one for another. And if any man hunger, let him eat at home; that ye come not together unto condemnation. And the rest will I set in order when I come."*

So nowhere in this particular situation does he rebuke the sin of drunkenness which he would have done if that was the actual problem. No, the issue was dealt with by his advice to eat and drink at home so as not to gather together to eat to capacity while others went without. He most certainly was not saying for them to go home in order that they may drink to the point of intoxication.

Paul would not contradict what he had said earlier in this same letter in chapter 5 and 6, which was to have no fellowship with a brother who was intoxicated through drinking too much wine but to rebuke him. But here in chapter 11, Paul teaches that the man concerned who had eaten and drunken *fully* to his own satisfaction while others went hungry should eat and drink at home rather than in the church.

Q. *But in Matthew 11:16-19 and Luke 7:31-34 the people of that generation accused Jesus of being a "wine-bibber" which means a tippler, lover of wine or a habitual drinker. The literal translation of the word means 'a drinker of oinos' (oinopotes). It says "For John came neither eating nor drinking, and they say, He hath a devil. The Son of man came eating and drinking, and they say, Behold a man gluttonous, and a winebibber, a friend of publicans and sinners." Does this not show that Jesus was in the habit of drinking alcoholic wine in normal life as well as in an environment with sinners? And if this is so is it not ok for us to do the same as a means of evangelism in going where sinners are in order to reach lost souls?*

A. That generation also accused Jesus in these verses of being a gluttonous man: one who overate and over-indulged in food. We know that this was not true. They took hold of the fact that He ate meat and declared Him a glutton. They also took hold of the fact that He drank wine which was unfermented grape juice and made Him a winebibber. This was another false accusation. Please notice that they did not call Him a drunkard but one who loved to habitually drink fermented wine—that is a social-drinker. The accusation that Christ was a social-drinker of alcohol was false and still is.

Jesus did not drink fermented wine to identify with the sinners of His generation neither did He go and sit in bars with sinners as a part of His social life. He came to reach lost sinners and He found the worst. In order to hear His message, Publicans (tax collectors) and sinners came and sat down with Him and His disciples when they were sitting eating in various homes and places (Mt.9:10-11; Lk.15:1-2). Also sinners and tax collectors who had already repented and believed His teachings sat with Him and as a result He was mocked (Lk.7:36-50; 19:7). This is why He was called a friend of sinners. The Pharisees wanted to infer that He was a friend of sinners in the sense of being a social companion and 'buddy' of practising sinners, as well as a social-drinker with them but this again was a false accusation based on twisted truth.

In these verses Jesus was condemning that generation for accusing John (the Baptist) of having a devil because he strictly did not drink wine or eat meat. He was also condemning them for implying that He (Jesus) was a glutton, social drinker and lover of intoxicating drink. I believe that today Jesus would also condemn those who mock teetotallers like John, or who make Jesus a supporter of social drinking. He has not changed.

The Scribes and Pharisees made the very same accusations against the Disciples of Christ, which were made against Christ Himself (Lk.5:29-30). We can be sure that many accusations will come against us but we must not be moulded by popular opinion, whether conservative or liberal. **We must rather be moulded by true biblical convictions.**

In verses 16 and 17 of Matthew and verses 31 and 32 of Luke Jesus gives a mini parable as a backdrop to understand all of these accusations. This is rarely, if ever, mentioned. He says this generation want you to dance when they pipe a tune and weep when they mourn. His parable teaches that this generation want you to conform to their latest contemporary conditions and customs. Christ is showing that you cannot win when dealing with contemporary culture. **They will either think you are too austere, like John, or too loose like Christ.**

The lesson in this is that we must mould our whole conduct before God, by the unchanging Word of God, and not by contemporary religious culture that changes with the wind.

Q. *In I Timothy 5:23, Paul writes to Timothy "Drink no longer water, but use a little wine for thy stomach's sake and thine often infirmities." Here is a clear command for a Christian to drink wine. I have frequently heard that a little alcoholic wine is good for the stomach. Is Paul not saying here that taking just a little alcoholic wine for a stomach complaint is ok? Surely this is one good reason?*

A. Before this instruction came from Paul, Timothy drank **neither** fermented nor unfermented wine. He abstained from both. Paul literally says here 'stop being strictly a water drinker only.' Timothy had not only practised abstinence from fermented wine prior to this but also abstained from unfermented wine as a drink. This was of course a stricter stance than any abstainer or teetotaller in our own day.

The reason Paul gives this advice is for the sake of Timothy's stomach. He was having some problem with his stomach and as a result it caused frequent feebleness. The cure was to take a little wine. Notice he said *"a little"* which can mean for a short period in the same way as a course of medicine is prescribed for a short period of time.

People laugh and joke about this scripture and use it as an encouragement to drink alcohol. However, it is quite clear that it was for a stomach problem, for a short time or as a little amount.

But most importantly you are right, many people do say that a little alcoholic wine is good for the stomach, but they are wrong. Even the medical profession say that a little alcoholic wine is good for the **heart** but the truth is that the 'good' ingredient in wine which is beneficial for the heart, called *resveratrol,* is higher in the content of purple grape juice than in fermented wine.

Also for the heart to gain any benefit from fermented wine, it would need to be drunk in such an amount that it would take the consumer passed the safe line of sobriety professed by social-drinkers. It would also have to be drunk in such an amount that the damaging side effects of the alcohol would damage other parts of the body. In other words, the disadvantages outweigh the advantages.

Please note however, **alcoholic wine is not advised by the medical profession for stomach problems**, in fact quite the opposite. Alcohol would tend to aggravate any stomach problems by inflaming the tissue of the stomach. Inflammation of the stomach tissue is not uncommon in moderate drinkers. Paul could only have been suggesting that Timothy drink grape juice, as it would settle the stomach.

The ancient Greek writers speak of 'stomach wine' or 'wine for the stomach.' This was a specific medicinal wine used for stomach complaints. It was **unfermented grape juice** and had no intoxicating effect whatsoever.

Pliny, Columella, Philo and others talked of many of their contemporary wines causing stomach problems. But

Athenaeus (end of second, beginning of third century Rhetorician), speaks of an alternative drink: "let him take sweet wine (*glukus*), either mixed with water or warmed, especially that called *protropos*, as being very good for the stomach."[24]

Q. *In the Parable of the Wineskin told by Jesus in Matthew 9, Mark 2 and Luke 5, we read of new wine being put into new wineskins in order to ferment. This shows that Jesus understood the process for fermenting wine and used this production of alcoholic wine as an example when teaching God's Word to people. If the wine was put into an old wineskin to ferment it would burst, but if put in a new wineskin it will expand to hold it safely. Surely this must show that He approved of making alcoholic wine and was maybe involved in such a process at some stage?*

A. You mention that new wine was placed in a new wineskin in order to ferment and that this process was revealed by the expanding of the wineskin. But I am afraid that is not correct. Elihu when speaking to Job and his friends in 32:19 says: *"Behold, my belly is as wine which hath no vent; it is ready to burst like new bottles."* Fermenting wine put in a new wineskin would burst the skin. It must have a vent or a means of releasing the carbonic gas. Such a process would expand the wine to **40 times more than its original size.**

Job reveals here that wine put in a new wineskin to ferment would burst. But if new wine was put in a new wineskin in order to preserve unfermented wine then it would simply mould the shape of the skin but not burst it. It should be very obvious that the term *new wine* must mean **un**fermented or non-alcoholic wine as that is in fact what the term 'new wine' means in the Bible. [For a further exposition on Christ's parable read about *Oinos* in chapter one].

Q. *We are told in Acts 2 that on the day of Pentecost: "Others mocking said, These men are full of new wine" to which Peter*

---

[24] Pg. 113, *Bible Wines or the Laws of Fermentation and the wines of the Ancients,* William Patton D.D. 1881. National Temperance Society and Publication House

responded: "For these are not drunken, as ye suppose, seeing it is but the third hour of the day" (2:13, 15). These inhabitants of Jerusalem were convinced that these disciples drank an intoxicating wine that could make them drunk. When Peter responds he does not deny that they drank intoxicating wine but only that the time of the day was wrong for drinking. If this accusation held no truth why did Peter not just state clearly that the followers of Christ did not drink intoxicating wine?

A. These mockers said that the Disciples were full of *"new Wine"*, which in Greek is *gleukos*. This is the only place in the New Testament where this word is used. Please note, that *oinos* (wine) is not used but a totally different word. *Oinos* was the most used word for wine in the New Testament and is a generic term that can describe fermented or unfermented wine, but *gleukos* conveys something very different and specific. It literally means sweet wine. **The process of fermentation changes all sugar in wine into alcohol and as a result can no longer be called *gleukos*.**

In the First Century, when Josephus wrote about Joseph's interpretation of the Butler's dream, and the fresh juice of the grape being squeezed into Pharaoh's cup, he called it *gleukos* (Gen.40:9-11). This means that in the First Century, Jews called freshly pressed juice of the grape that was free of fermentation *gleukos*.

When Jerome, in the Fourth Century, came to translate these scriptures into Latin he used the word *musto* for *gleukos*. From *musto* we get our English word *'must'* which always and only means unfermented grape juice, or unfermented wine. *Must* is a drink which is totally free from fermentation. This is why Wycliffe and other gifted Bible translators in the 16th Century translated this verse into English as, *"these men ben ful of must."*

From this we see that these mockers were saying that the Disciples of Christ were full to the brim of sweet, unfermented wine. These followers of Christ were well known for drinking *gleukos*, which was fully understood by Jews of that day to be unfermented wine. These mockers knew exactly what they were saying when they used the word *gleukos*.

Please note, that these mockers **were not asking a sincere question** neither were they confused over the facts; they were making a statement to mock the Disciples. They were saying that these men who only drink sweet grape juice have drunk so much that they are intoxicated. It was pure ridicule and mockery. No doubt these mockers were social drinkers who took opportunity to ridicule this practice at every opportunity.

Peter stands up and responds by saying, *"For these are not drunken* [methuo], *as ye suppose, seeing it is but the third hour of the day."* Remember that the word *methuo* does not only mean intoxication but also to drink until you are full, or to drink until you are fully satisfied. Peter is saying that it is only nine o' clock in the morning and no man has drunk his fill of sweet new wine by that time in the morning, never mind any intoxicating wine. He is answering the mocking with a simple fact of reality. He then goes on to explain that this is what Joel spoke of concerning the outpouring of the Spirit.

Peter in his later epistles calls all Christians to a life of total abstinence from drinking fermented wine (*nepho*). This again confirms that it was the practice, conviction and example of Peter to only drink pure grape juice.

Q. *In Philippians 4:5 Paul says: "Let your moderation be known unto all men. The Lord is at hand." It would seem that Paul is clearly saying here that the practice of moderation in drinking alcohol is a Christian virtue expected of every believer. We should be known to all men to be moderate in all things that we do. Extreme abstinence is not commanded but moderation is. A careful, conscientious, self-controlled use of alcohol is expected. What is your response to this?*

A. There is nothing in the context of this passage which should make us imagine that Paul means we should be moderate in drinking alcohol. **Alcohol has nothing to do with this verse.** In fact the Greek word *epieikes* means suitable, mild, gentle, reasonableness or forbearance. It is translated elsewhere as *"patience"* (I Tim.3:3) and *"gentle"* (Tit.3:2; Jm.3:17; I Pet.2:18). **It is speaking about a character not an action**. It is an inward virtue, not an outward habit.

The moderation mentioned here has nothing whatsoever to do with the practice of only drinking a little alcohol, in a careful balanced manner. Social drinkers speak about drinking in moderation but it has nothing to do with this verse and there is no teaching in the Bible which instructs us to drink alcohol moderately. The so-called 'moderation doctrine' is presently doing much harm to the Church and has repeatedly failed in what it claims to do.

Other Questions

Q. *I have read a number of reports in reliable papers and magazines in recent years reporting medical and scientific evidence and data from top doctors and scientists concerning the many health properties and benefits contained in red wine when drunk in moderation. How do you explain this?*

A. You are correct, the media periodically and widely reports the health benefits of red wine in connection to the health of the heart; in having properties that retard aging and which promote general health. All of this is presented and supported by professional medical personnel. But there is actually no verified or undisputed evidence to support this.

For example: Dr. Dipak K. Das, PhD, a researcher and director at the University of Connecticut's Cardiovascular Research Centre, conducted in-depth research into the health benefits of red wine. He was one of the main persons behind the reports which promoted the health benefits of red wine for the heart, and until 2008, he led research on *resveratrol*.

Although grants are difficult to get he received two governmental grants worth a total of $890,000. It seems that funds flowed freely to the Doctor because of the type of research he was conducting and the results he produced. His research also won him financial gain from various businesses and companies involved in the sale of red wine.

His research produced 26 articles published in 11 different journals. One report reads, "Das, was a prolific publisher of research. His name appears on over 500 articles, including 117 articles on *resveratrol*..." All of this material was published since the year, 2000, with one report of his successful research appearing in the *New York Times*.

However, an investigation of the Doctor's work began in January 2009 after the University received an anonymous allegation concerning the irregularities of his work. After a three year investigation covering just seven years of his research work, Dr Das was found guilty in January, 2012, of **145 counts of fabrication or falsification of data**. The investigation body decided to stop at 145 counts, although his misdemeanours greatly exceeded that. As a result the grants were recalled and he was dismissed from his department.

David Sinclair, a Harvard biologist, who is the best-known person in *resveratrol* research, told the *New York Times* that he had never heard of Dr. Das and that his exposure would have little effect upon this vital research. However, it turns out that Mr. Sinclair had been on a committee with Das and had cited him in articles. Another researcher and Harvard psychologist, Marc Hauser, resigned in 2011, after being found guilty of similar 'irregularities' in his research.

This is the sort of false, secular, popular propaganda which gets widely promoted as fact concerning the virtue of red fermented wine and which sticks in the minds of many in spite of the exposure of the false. Sadly many Christians believe such false research and reports, then promote these lies in support of their Christian social-drinking habits. Need I say more?

Q. *Is unfermented wine or grape juice good for your health?*

A. It most certainly is. Just read the following comment from expert Doctor, John D. Folts, Ph.D., who is the director of the Coronary Thrombosis Research Laboratory, at the University of Wisconsin Medical School USA. He is an internationally recognised researcher specialising in the effect of diet in relation to coronary artery disease.

> "Concord grape juice has more than three times the naturally occurring antioxidants of orange, grapefruit, apple or tomato juice, and twice as much per serving as the 42 other tested fruits and vegetables...in well-

designed preliminary clinical research, drinking Concord grape juice reduced the tendency of platelets in the blood to clump together, helping to maintain the free flow of blood in the arteries...Wine and Concord grape juice appear to be significant platelet inhibitors, meaning they make the platelets in the blood less likely to clot."

HEART—UK, a leading cholesterol charity, has officially recognised *Welch's* Purple Grape Juice for its abundant antioxidant properties and role in promoting heart health. It is the first time a 100% pure and unsweetened juice has received the coveted HEART—UK approval. These are just the beginnings of recent medical and scientific discoveries concerning unfermented wine.

It is no wonder then that the Bible promotes wine (grape juice) more than any other drink but warns against and condemns the drinking of alcoholic drinks. The Bible is simply backed up and confirmed by recent medical and scientific research.

Q. *I believe that this discussion concerning alcohol amongst Christians is purely cultural. For example, there is a history of abstinence in America and Britain but this does not exist in many European countries and in fact the church in these European nations practise social drinking as a normal, healthy part of local culture.*

It is a well known fact that France which has a long history of wine drinking handles its drinking habits wisely and teaches its young people to drink in a family environment. They are taught how to drink wine and they do so at meal times. Socially France has fewer problems related to alcohol than those seen in America or Britain. In fact, the French have a very low rate of heart disease due to drinking wine and their alcohol addiction problem is limited in comparison to other nations. This has been a normal part of the practice of the Church in France, which sees no contradiction between drinking wine and a life of holiness.

A. This view concerning Europe and especially France is popular, but it is terribly misleading. Kenneth L. Gentry in his book, *God Gave Wine*, written in defence of social drinking, uses the argument that the French have a very low rate of heart problems.[25] **What he does not tell you is the tragic impact that wine has upon the nation.**

France is one of the three leading producers of wine in the world, and has the highest consumption rate in the world. French children learn to drink at a young age, often at home, and as a result the French are the heaviest drinking nation in the world.

The fruit of this is that France has **twice the rate of cirrhosis of the liver** as North America. Each year 15% of deaths in France are attributed to chronic liver disease and cirrhosis. In 1980 it was **30% of the nation's deaths.** This has only dropped in the past three decades because of serious warnings made to the French population concerning their traditional, cultural drinking habits. But the problem is not limited to health.

Official French statistics tell us that 40% of traffic accidents which result in death are due to alcohol consumption. That is 4,000 deaths a year. There are numberless other tragic consequences of alcohol in France: mentally, physically, morally and of course spiritually.

Sadly, you are right when it comes to drinking amongst those in the French churches—it has become the culture of the Church in France, and indeed other European nations to drink socially, but Church history in France reveals a very different story. Over the past 130 years, the two main Christian movements to impact and pioneer in France were the Salvation Army, under the leadership of the Arthur and Katie Booth-Clibborn, and the Pentecostal movement, under the leadership of Douglas Scott. The history of their pioneering work in France is nothing less than dynamic, militant, successful evangelism birthed in a true spirit of revival. These movements won multitudes to Christ and pioneered many new churches. **Both movements practised and taught total abstinence.**

Much more could be said on this subject, but the above should be sufficient to prove that when France, or other European wine-producing, wine-drinking nations, are held up as

---

[25] p.137, *God Gave Wine* K.L. Gentry

a positive example, it just proves that those doing so, know little about the **actual facts**. Italy, for example, has the most serious problem with drunk-driving by youths of any country in Europe, but such cultures and their customs of wine drinking are being presented as an example for the Church to follow. This is utter foolishness, not to mention, seriously dangerous. **The Church has its own culture and that culture is the culture of Christ as taught clearly in the New Testament.**

Q. *In order to reach people in the world I believe I must go into their homes, pub's, discos or wherever they are and will even have a casual drink with them in order to win them over to Jesus and the church. We must identify with today's young culture. Jesus would have done the same. The world thinks we are different and that is why they do not come to Church. We must be relevant, innovative and progressive in our methods and style. Of course we present the same unchanging message but to reach the world you must be like the world. Methodology does not matter. If that means drinking a beer, turning the church into a pub or turning worship into a disco, then it is ok as long as our motive is to win people to Jesus. Surely that is ok?*

A. Paul says in Romans 12:2: *"And be **not** conformed to this world:"* The word *"conformed"* means to be fashioned like it; to conform to its pattern; to be pressed into its image. The common teaching of today's church is: 'Be conformed to this world.' This is confusion and disobedience to the Word of God.

I Peter 4:2-4, speaks of this very thing and warns that if a true Christian separates himself from his previous worldly desires of drinking, partying, carousing and the like, that those of this world will, *"think it strange that ye run not with them to the same excess of riot, speaking evil of you:"*

Again Paul speaks of those in the world in Ephesians 5:7-8 *"Be not ye therefore partakers with them. For ye were sometimes darkness, but now are ye light in the Lord: walk as children of light:"* And in 5:11 *"And have no fellowship with the unfruitful works of darkness, but rather reprove them."*

We do not have even one good, profitable example anywhere in the Bible of followers of the Lord following the ways or practices of the world in order to win the world over to God's truth—not one. The power of the early Church was like that of Samson of old—it depended upon utter separation from the world and sanctification by the Holy Spirit. When the church was separate from the world it had power over the world but once it compromised holy convictions, it lost its power to reach towns, cities, nations and continents with the gospel of Jesus Christ.

When you see church youth or leadership groups meeting in pubs; churches rebuilt to look like pubs, and a general conformity to the looks, sounds and actions of the world you can be sure that the world has succeeded in evangelizing the church with its gospel of 'eat, drink and be happy.'

Q. *Drinking alcohol is just like eating food or having sex. All these things can be sinful. It is not the fact of using them that is wrong but how you use them. It is the abuse of them, not the use of them. Eating food is not sinful but eating too much is sinful. We don't abstain from food we eat it in moderation. If we applied the principles you teach to sex it would mean that we would have to abstain from all sexual relationships because it is frequently abused in our world. How do you reconcile this?*

A. Firstly, you are not applying this principle correctly. Eating, drinking and sex should only be used in line with the specific and full teaching of the Word of God concerning them i.e.: we should only use them as the Bible teaches us how to use them.

Sex is only ok within the boundary of Scripture which teaches that it is between one man and one woman within the marriage bond. Sex within these parameters is ok; fornication, adultery, homosexuality and polygamy are not. All other forms of sex outside of marriage must be totally abstained from.

Food is handled in the same way. It is not abstinence from all food without qualification, but too much food is gluttony and therefore, sin. Some food will hurt and damage the physical body and if one is wise and believes what the Bible teaches one should totally abstain from it.

The same goes for drink; I am not teaching that we abstain from all drinks. The Bible mentions water, milk and other drinks which are strongly encouraged. Neither am I saying that we should abstain from all wine (*yayin* or *oinos*). I am however strongly teaching that we totally abstain from all fermented wine. This is the clear teaching of the whole of Scriptures and I am operating within it when I abstain from all intoxicating drinks.

Q. *I have heard repeatedly that the teaching of total abstinence from all alcoholic drinks is only about 150 years old and that previous to that time the church both ancient and modern had never heard of it. It supposedly began in North America with the Temperance Movement which initially only promoted abstinence from spirits and moderation in drinking wine and beer. This was further strengthened when Dr. T.B. Welch (1825-1903) began producing his unfermented wine in 1869 for the first time in history. He then promoted the use of his unfermented wine for communion in churches. Is the teaching on abstinence that you are presenting here a North American 19th Century invention?*

A. No not at all. It is most certainly not a 19th Century invention, nor is it a North American invention. Anyone who says so reveals their ignorance of Church and secular history.

After the close of the Canon of Scripture we have various writers in the Church who made a clear stand against drinking intoxicating beverages and commended believers to abstinence; writers such as Clement of Alexandria (150-215 AD), and Jerome (346-420 AD). In the first four centuries, there were various spiritual movements and leaders who abstained and who did not use fermented wine at the Lord's Table.

In more recent centuries, we only have to look back to the beginning of the Reformation in Europe to find a constant flow of spiritual movements and leaders who held fast to the biblical teaching of abstinence from alcohol. It was these movements which carried their teachings to America where such truths became an established part of holy conviction in the various revivals which then impacted secular society and politics in greater and greater degrees during the 19th Century, eventually leading to the abolition of alcohol in America in the early 20th Century.

Amongst the groups, movements or churches after the Reformation which did allow the drinking of fermented wine or beer were a number of very good men (see chapter 9: *Alcohol, Reformation and Revival*). They walked in the light they had at that time with its own limitations and restrictions. But one thing to note is that even those who were not abstainers were very strong and constant in their warnings, preaching and teaching against its great dangers. This is utterly missing from those churches who promote social drinking today.

If you read secular histories concerning the state of American society before the Temperance movement began, you will see that some drastic measure was desperately needed. Alcohol was destroying the strength, health and morality of the nation. It called for drastic action and the Church with its spiritual revivals was the morale influence behind this. During the 19th Century, Temperance movements and societies started up in many other nations but this most certainly was not the beginning of the biblical teaching on abstinence.

Many great men taught total abstinence before the 19th Century and even used unfermented wine for communion long before Dr Welch started producing his unfermented wine at the end of the 19th Century. As it happens Welch only rediscovered what was an ancient art of taking freshly pressed grape juice, heating it to 60°C (140°F), to kill the wild yeasts and to prevent any fermentation from taking place.

Now, once again in the USA, we see a growing problem in secular society. Those who are 21 years old and younger consume a quarter of all alcohol in the nation. No other substance is threatening American youth as much as alcohol. Sadly, in an hour when the nation is plunging into moral darkness the Church has lost its abstinence conviction and instead is on a crusade to convert abstainers to social drinking with a constant assault of misquotes; scriptures taken out of context, inaccurate presentations and false perceptions of Church history as demonstrated by your question.

Before we touch the nation again we must convince the preachers and leaders of our churches that the Bible teaches abstinence. They in turn must teach the people and as a result reach out to a lost world with a gospel that totally delivers from every intoxicating drink.

Q. *Using the word temperance for abstaining from alcohol is not correct. According to its biblical use to be temperate carries the meaning of being disciplined, careful and controlled. When used in connection with drinking alcohol its correct meaning is to use alcohol in a careful, controlled and monitored manner. It does not mean to abstain. What is your response?*

A. The word *"temperance"* or *"temperate"* is used four times in our English Bible (Acts 24:25; Gal.5:22-23; II Pet.1:5-6; I Cor.9:25). It literally means **self-control**. It is one of the fruit of the Holy Spirit which manifests in the action of mastering your desires, passions and appetites in bringing them under the control of the Holy Spirit and the written scriptures. Because *"drunkenness"* is spoken of as a manifestation of the flesh, the word temperance was used by those who believed in total abstinence and it was they who called the Church to return to this biblical teaching. True temperance will keep the body free from any substance condemned by the teaching of the scriptures.

Q. *While I agree with you that all Christians should abstain from intoxicating drinks and that this is the best and most perfect way for the individual, the church and the glory of God, I do however believe that the wine Jesus drank had a very small percentage of alcohol; maybe 3 or 4% and that it was frequently diluted with water. I think when we deny such clear simple facts concerning Christ drinking wine with some alcohol content, that social drinkers do not take us seriously and we lose our credibility. As a result they simply won't listen.*

Also if we infer that drinking a moderate amount of alcohol occasionally is a sin we will only alienate social drinkers to a place where we cannot reason with them to forsake alcohol for the good of all and will also bring division amongst genuine believers. Is this what you desire?

A. Men like, Peter Masters in England and, John MacArthur in America, abstain from alcohol themselves and teach abstinence, yet go on to teach the theory that Jesus drank wine with some percentage of alcohol. While I am glad that these men teach abstinence, I am amazed that they believe that Jesus drank wine with a percentage of alcohol.

This does much damage to trying to persuade social drinkers to abstain. It is a very weak argument. To teach abstinence yet admit that Christ drank wine which was fermented undermines an abstinence position.

To say that the wine Christ and His disciples drank had a low percentage of alcohol or was mixed with water carries no biblical or historical proof at all. There is no evidence for this. It is a mere supposition, not a fact.

As far as 'losing credibility' with social drinkers is concerned, indeed the opposite is true. To tell them that Jesus drank wine with a small percentage of alcohol, yet advise them to abstain totally from it, is a contradiction and will not carry weight with most convinced social drinkers. If Jesus and the Disciples did drink some element of alcohol, then why would contemporary Christians who drink socially abstain? If Jesus drank it, then they should be permitted to drink it.

The fable that Jesus partook of low alcohol wine does not and will not encourage abstinence. There are multitudes that attend churches yet drink beer who do not even consider that they are really drinkers. Why is this? The average contemporary beer has only 3 or 4% of alcohol content and so they consider that low alcoholic drinks do not fall into the bracket of real drinking and certainly are in no way condemned in the Bible. Although this reasoning may seem foolish to some it is in fact the very thought of many.

You also mention that calling social drinking a sin will alienate us from those whom we may influence for good and 'bring division between genuine believers' but **we cannot base unity or division on an issue like social drinking**. We must make our stand upon the clear teaching of the Word of God and persuade genuine believers to return to the revelation of God's Word. Even if a leader seems sincere and genuine, we cannot change the written Word for him. A real believer will always be most impressed by a clear exposition of the Word of God.

We can walk in fellowship and unity of faith with all believers who are sound in the fundamentals of the faith. Upon this basis and within these boundaries, we should continue to use biblical persuasion, ministered humbly, clearly and convincingly to those with whom we disagree. Charles Spurgeon began his ministry as a convinced social drinker, but finished in total support of total abstinence. Good men in this generation need to be convinced of the biblical truth of abstinence.

Q. *Am I not correct in saying that C.H. Spurgeon the great gospel preacher of the Metropolitan Tabernacle in London drunk fermented wine and strong drink? I believe that he made a clear stand in contending that it was a part of his liberty in Christ and refused to give an inch on the habit of drinking alcohol for the sake of the Gospel. No one could doubt how mightily God used him or his profound knowledge of the Bible.*

A. No matter how great a man of God Spurgeon was, that is no reason for us to believe that he was correct or indeed an example to follow. Down through the ages, great men have had certain *things* wrong, yet the Lord used them. Spurgeon was undoubtedly one of the great gospel preachers of Church history, but in his early years he was certainly wrong on this issue.

But even during these earliest years of ministry, although not an abstainer, he made it clear that he respected abstainers, hated drunkenness as much as any other man, and that he would stand shoulder to shoulder with abstainers in the war against drunkenness and intemperance.[26]

In, 1877, he wrote in his publication, *The Sword and the Trowel,* that he had read a book by A.M. Wilson which proved to him that there was no such thing as unfermented wine in Bible days, and that such a thought was a myth. He goes on to state: "Mr. Wilson has written the thick volume now before us to settle the matter, and we believe that he establishes beyond reasonable debate that the wines of the Bible were intoxicating, and that our

---

[26] September, 1857

Lord did not ordain jelly or syrup, or cherry juice to be the emblem of his sacrifice."[27]

But by March 1882, when writing a personal letter to the first Tabernacle Total Abstinence Society at the time of its formation he was able to say: "**Next to the preaching of the Gospel, the most necessary thing to be done in England is to induce our people to become abstainers.**"[28] This new society had his full backing and encouragement. What a strong, definite change in a five year period!

Two years later when writing to the Temperance Society he said: "I hope they will be full of spirit against evil spirits, stout against stout, and hale against ale."[29]

By 1887 he was proudly wearing the blue ribbon of the temperance movement and supporting its cause in the nation. He was also able to write in that year that at the Metropolitan Tabernacle they used only unfermented wine and he defined such wine as "the pure juice of the grape."[30] Furthermore, Temperance meetings were held in the church and he was able to say with personal conviction: "I abstain myself from alcoholic drink in every form, and I think others would be wise to do the same; but of this each one must be a guide unto himself."[31] Until his death he continued as a vital supporter of this vital cause of abstinence.

This should give us strong hope that genuine and sincere believers who presently believe in social drinking, may be won over as we patiently present the truth of God's Word in a clear, convincing, gracious manner without calling them names, mocking them or ostracising them.

Q. *Is there not a 'demon of alcohol' which is why so many come under the influence of alcohol and cannot get free? I think Alcoholics need deliverance from this demon and it's just a pity that there are not enough Deliverance ministries around to perform this.*

---

[27] p. 437, *The Sword and the Trowel*, 1877.
[28] p. 440, *Spurgeon: Prince of Preachers*, Lewis Drummond
[29] Letter to *Temperance Society*, March 19, 1884
[30] June 20, 1887.
[31] *The Waterpots at Cana*, C.H. Spurgeon

A. No, there is no actual demon of alcohol. We never once see a demon of alcohol being cast out of anyone in the New Testament by Christ or the apostles. In fact as we have already seen drunkenness is clearly taught to be a sin of the flesh or manifestation of the flesh, not a demon (Gal.5:19-21). In the New Testament drunkenness is constantly called a soul damming sin and Paul gives us very clear instructions on how to deal with such people and minister to them but never once does he suggest casting a demon out of them.

For the unsaved person, alcohol addiction most certainly opens up his life to many influences, not least of a spiritual nature. There can be no doubt that alcohol and drunkenness are weapons in the devils armoury. By this means Satan seeks to keep people from true salvation. But we do not need more so-called Deliverance ministries. Instead we need more old-fashioned Gospel preaching which brings a conviction of sin and brings the alcoholic to true repentance. We need more teaching which declares the power of the blood of Jesus to set a repentant alcoholic free.

For the truly born-again believer who has repented and been washed in the blood there is no indwelling demon of alcohol. He is free. Yes he can be tempted, harassed and buffeted but not demonized. But social drinking can indeed give the devil a foothold in his life or a stronghold in his mind. If a man embraces social drinking and goes on to cross the line numerous times, the Devil then has ground in his life from which he will wage a war against him. The drinker will then be condemned by the accusation of his enemy and rightfully so. *"Ye cannot drink the cup of the Lord, and the cup of devils: ye cannot be partakers of the Lord's Table and of the table of devils"* (I Cor.10:21).

Let us be clear: **alcohol is not a demon in a bottle waiting to possess the unsuspecting.** The desire for enjoying the effects of alcohol comes from the flesh of man. The Devil does not have to work very hard when our own fallen natures err naturally toward 'products of the fall'. We must not blame the devil for alcohol addiction or sins that arise from social-drinking. We must preach the truth of God clearly and call saint and sinner alike to repent.

Q. *But it does seem evident that many people are born into a family with a GENERATIONAL CURSE of alcoholism hanging over them and as a result they grow up as victims of this cursed addiction. Alcoholism is passed down through the family line and as a result certain people are more prone to it than others. Does this curse need broken from off you if your parents or grandparents were alcoholics?*

A. Exodus 34:7 tells us that God *"...will by no means clear the guilty; visiting the iniquity of the fathers upon the children, and upon the children's children, unto the third and to the fourth generation"* and Lamentations 5:7 says: *"Our fathers have sinned, and are not; and we have borne their iniquities."* Scripture is clear in its teaching that the sins of parents can have a terrible effect down to the third or fourth generation. The consequence, influence and affect of the sins of one generation are passed on to the next. This has been true from the beginning of time. Adam's sin has affected all of us.

But take good note as to who these sins are visited upon. It is those who hate him (Ex.20:5), the guilty (34:7; Num.14:18) and those who stir up the jealousy of God by their personal sin (Deut.5:9).

There has also certainly been much teaching in the Church of recent decades concerning the blessings and curses contained in Deuteronomy 28. It has become normal practice to find or discern what curse is still affecting the life of a born-again believer. Prayers are then prayed over the person in order to break this curse; the person concerned must renounce the sins of his fathers, and strange chopping hand movements are made in order to set the person free from these generational curses.

The curses of Deuteronomy 28 were instituted as part of the Jewish legal system. It was a vital part of that process of seeking to fulfil the law of righteousness by means of your own efforts and works in order to attain perfect righteousness. Paul teaches much in the book of **Romans** concerning two different types of righteousness. One was received at salvation by grace through faith in the finished work of the Cross. But the other was a law of righteousness which could only be attained by keeping the law perfectly. If a Jew was to break one law at one single point he would no longer be perfectly righteous and he would then be under the curse of the law.

The teaching of curses only appears once in the New Testament and it is in this very context of either accepting the perfect righteousness of Christ by faith as a gift or ignoring this perfect righteousness and following a pathway by which one goes about to establish his own righteousness by his own good deeds.

"For as many as are of the works of the law are under the curse: for it is written, Cursed is every one that continueth not in all things which are written in the book of the law to do them. But that no man is justified by the law in the sight of God, it is evident: for, The just shall live by faith. And the law is not of faith: but, The man that doeth them shall live in them. Christ hath redeemed us from the curse of the law, being made a curse for us: for it is written, Cursed is every one that hangeth on a tree:" (Galatians 3:10-13)

The curse of the law which results from failing to fulfil and keep each law by not walking perfectly before God has been dealt with at the Cross. Here you have a choice: Will you attempt to keep the law and suffer the consequences of the curse, if you fail, or will you put your faith in the finished work of the Cross alone and receive the perfect righteousness of Christ as the only means of pleasing God and as the foundation of your walk with God?

The teaching of 'blessings and curses' taught in the contemporary Church of our day is nothing less than Old Testament legalism. Nowhere in the *Book of Acts* do we see the Apostles or churches going through a ritual of breaking generational curses. Neither do you find this teaching in the *Epistles*. The born-again believer washed in the blood who walks with God in a loving friendship is free from the curse.

Balaam could not curse Israel while they walked with God. Only when they sinned and turned from obedience to God did the Lord punish them. Sin is not the result of a curse but the result of the fall of Adam. Where a sinful act or trait is found in the life it must be repented of. A sinful trait is no evidence of a generational curse in the family.

CHAPTER 12
CHRIST, WINE AND ALCOHOL

Did Jesus Drink Wine? Yes—He most certainly did. The Bible says so. But did He drink wine containing alcohol? That is the real question we should be asking. Did Jesus promote the social drinking of alcohol? Or did he abstain from taking any drink which contained alcohol?

One of the most commonly repeated, promoted and pressed comments by those seeking to justify social drinking, or the moderate drinking of alcohol, is that '**Christ turned water into wine.**' Sinner and Saint alike use this simple comment to justify their love of alcohol. It has become a motto, national anthem, unquestioned statement of faith, and an unanswerable proclamation—or so they think.

By simply stating that 'Christ turned the water into wine' the social drinker assumes that the wine was fermented and that this fermented drink had the potential, if taken in a large enough quantity, to make a man drunk. By this they infer that Christ promotes, encourages, aids and blesses the moderate, social drinking of wine and other fermented drinks.

Most of those who repeat this oft used statement do not know where to find it in their Bibles. Most who repeat it have not given any personal thought or study to the subject. It has become a habitual practice to pass on this comment which has been heard thousands of times throughout their lives. Such a habit forms the heart, foundation and core of popular heresies, fables and general nonsense.

This book has tested such fables and popular, unhelpful comments concerning wine and alcohol—tested by the written Word of God—and these tests have found them utterly lacking in any biblical foundation. In this last chapter, we shall set wine, alcohol, social drinking and drunkenness in the full context of the person of Jesus Christ.

Most who have promoted social drinking have done so on the basis that Christ not only made wine but drank wine as well. Although very few would dare say that Christ would drink to a point of intoxication, almost all assume that He drank wine that had **the potential to intoxicate.**

For this very reason, we must make the Bible's teaching concerning Christ, wine and alcohol to be the capstone of all that we have said so far. Every teaching of the Bible must be seen in its right context through the person of Christ.

Although we have already explained that Christ made **unfermented wine** at Cana, in our last chapter we will revisit it as we look at Christ and wine.

First Miracle

After thirty years of obscurity, Christ came to the banks of the Jordan to be baptised by John, to be commended by His Heavenly Father, and to be anointed by the Holy Ghost for His short ministry.

For the next three and a half years, He would be intensively and consistently in the public eye, under religious scrutiny for any mistake in word or deed, and would be watched by His personal, intimate disciples who would then record and follow His practice, principles, habits, convictions, example and teachings.

In John Chapter two, we read that Christ and His disciples were *"called"*, or invited, to the marriage feast at Cana in Galilee which was about 8 ½ miles north of Nazareth. Later in the same Gospel we read that Nathanael, one of the twelve, was from Cana (Jn.21:2). It was just before this first miracle that Nathanael became a follower of Jesus Christ (Jn.1:45-51).

Jesus' mother, Mary, seemed to have some organizational function at this wedding. She was already there, she took responsibility for the wine when it ran out, and she was able to instruct the servants to follow Christ's commands.

This joyous marriage was the place chosen for Christ to begin a ministry that would reveal His Messiah-ship and Divinity. *"This beginning of miracles did Jesus in Cana of Galilee, and manifested forth his glory"* (2:11). A miracle is simply a sign which points to something: it is a signal that indicates a message. It was a spiritual truth revealed by a physical miracle.

While the only message the contemporary Church usually emphasise from this miracle is that they have the right to drink fermented wine, the truth is something very different. This miracle *"manifested forth his glory"* to all gathered; a glory which He had with the Father in eternity past. It revealed the truth of His divinity; He was God and He was the Creator of all things (Jn.1:1-3, 10; Eph.3:9; Col.1:16; Heb.1:12; Gen.1:1; Rev.4:10).

The One who created all things at the *Beginning*, was now standing in Cana and could do the very same thing. He created the vine and the process which led to the growth of its grapes. **In nature, what He had created to take a period of months, Christ now accomplished miraculously in just moments.** In nature the vine draws water from the ground and turns it into juice-filled grapes on the branch. The contents of the water pots in Cana were filled with water but were miraculously turned into new wine—fresh grape juice. By this means He showed forth His eternal glory.

This miracle did not contradict the perfection of His creation order. Christ had the power to either turn the water into wine that would weaken and numb the mental and emotional powers, which could intoxicate and which was the cause of constant harm and damage, or He could make wine which was new, fresh, refreshing, stimulating, healthy and free from any intoxicating influence.

The Christ of creation would not damage the human body. He would never make, provide and give a drink which would undermine the mental and physical senses which He gave man in creation.

The fermentation process which turns new wine, into intoxicating wine, is part of the fall of man. **It is a process of decay.** When wine is freshly pressed it is free of ferment. When Christ multiplied the seven loaves and few little fish for the multitudes to eat, He did not create mouldy bread or rotten fish. It was fresh. He also created new wine without fermentation.

Public ministry
This miracle of turning water into wine was the first miracle which Christ performed after being anointed with the Holy Ghost in the River Jordan. Some would have us believe that this anointing of power enabled Him to create an intoxicating drink for an already drunken wedding party.

The truth is the exact opposite. Christ was anointed of the Holy Ghost to cure the ills caused by alcohol in Jewish society. Christ brought the cure for the curse alcohol brings. This miracle did not contradict His commission to deliver and heal men:

- *"...he hath sent me to bind up the brokenhearted".* Alcohol is the cause of broken hearts and untold heartache which only Christ can bind up.
- *"to proclaim liberty to the captives".* Alcohol has placed many in captivity under its addictive power from which Christ alone can set at liberty.
- *"and the opening of the prison to them that are bound".* Alcohol has made untold multitudes prisoners to this terrible addiction but Christ alone has the power to open the prison doors and release them from all bondage (Isa.61:1; Lk.4:18-19). Alcohol has also literally put multitudes behind prison bars as a result of criminal acts.

Thank God that Christ has changed many and they have not been back in prison.

This anointing and power of the Holy Spirit did not aid the heartbreaking, binding, captivating influence of alcohol but rather came to break it from off hurting humanity. **Christ would** not fuel the practice of drinking, whilst healing and delivering those afflicted by it. **This would be an act of removing the bad fruit while encouraging the growth of the bad root.**

When Christ came ministering publically many false accusations were made against Him, such as that of being a devil, of being mad and of being a gluttonous man. Another false accusation was that of being a *"winebibber"* (Mt.11:19; Lk.7:34). A *"winebibber"* (*oinopotes*) was one who could *quickly down a pint*. It literally and simply means a tippler or a drinker of wine. It consists of two words: *oinos,* our word for wine, and *pino,* our word for drink. A winebibber was a *habitual* drinker of wine. No mention of amount is revealed by this word but only the fact that it was a consistent habit. **A winebibber was not a drunkard but a social drinker.** Only fermented wine can be meant by this term for it alone is condemned throughout the Bible.

According to the Mishna, a collection of Jewish writings from about 200 AD, a **drunkard was one who drank a quarter of a pint of wine** which is not much in comparison to what drinkers consume today. This would be equivalent to what a moderate or social drinker would consume in our own day.

The false accusation that Christ was a winebibber (if believed) would damage His reputation and teaching ministry. To call Him a winebibber was an attempt to blacken His character, to blemish His good testimony, and to hinder His ministry. But since it was a false accusation, Christ did not even respond to it.

So, on one hand we have Christ falsely called a winebibber because He drank the pure unfermented juice of the grape, and on the other hand we have John the Baptist accused of having a devil because he abstained from all wine. These two accusations are still made within today's Church. A great many still accuse Christ of being a social drinker of intoxicating wine, and the very same people accuse abstainers of having a legalistic demon.

Social drinkers would say that Christ was a moderate, controlled drinker who never got drunk; but this is the very accusation which was made against Christ when He walked the streets of Jerusalem. This was a damaging accusation in those days, but now it has been transformed to be the embodiment and emblem of **Christian liberty.** In Christ's day to be a habitual drinker of intoxicating wine was enough to ruin your reputation if in ministry; now it is the mark of orthodoxy.

Christ fulfilled the Old Testament prophecies, types and shadows but also fulfilled three realms of ministry as Prophet, Priest and King. This was not part-time ministry for Christ. His whole earthly life (and now heavenly life) was caught up in this threefold ministry. He was never free from it.

As Prophet, Christ was to be the voice of God, the mouthpiece of God, revealing the mind, thought and will of God. Some would have us to believe that He drank intoxicating wine during His public preaching tours and taught the people in homes over a fermented bottle of wine. No—Christ walked in the godly line of Old Testament prophets like Jeremiah, Amos and so many others. They did not abstain from unfermented wine but from wine that had gone through the process of fermentation. The prophets constantly dealt with the sin of the people in relation to alcohol.

As our Great High Priest who stands between God and man, He had to be free from every intoxicating influence. It was not sufficient to remain free from drunkenness; He could not approach His Heavenly Father on our behalf if there was any influence of drink whatsoever upon Him. Christ fulfilled this and still does.

As the King and the promised Messiah of Israel, He fulfilled and obeyed King Solomon's instruction in Proverbs 31 that *"it is not for kings to drink wine; nor for princes strong drink."* He was also the Prince of Peace. This royal Heavenly King walked free from all influence of fermented wine and strong drink. He never willingly put a cup of fermented juice to His lips.

In His humanity He walked in all the Word of God spoken of in the Old Testament Scriptures. He came to fulfil them, not destroy them. When Solomon gave the instruction that fermented wine should not be *looked upon,* Jesus fulfilled it. He was not a rebel against the written Word but an example of one who fulfilled it and who made such teachings honourable once more. In every realm of life and ministry He walked perfectly before His Heavenly Father and this most certainly included abstinence from all intoxicating drinks.

His Teachings

In His teachings Christ frequently mentioned vineyards, the vine, wine, fruit of the vine and wineskins (Jn.15; Mt.20:1-16; 21:28-41; Mk.12:1-9; Lk.20:9-16). In the Old Testament, the nation of Israel was always pictured as the vine of God (Ps.80; Isa.5; Jer.2:21; 12:10; Hos.10:1). These Scriptures constantly speak of Israel's failure as the vine of God and the judgement with which she would be judged. But there is also the promise that the Lord would raise up another vine unto Himself (Ps.80:17). When we come to the teachings of Christ in the New Testament, He again portrays Israel as the Lord's vineyard and adds some serious warnings (Mt.21:33-46).

But Christ not only knew and understood the prophecies concerning Israel as the vine of God He also understood the full teaching of the Old Testament in relation to what it taught concerning wine, strong drink and drunkenness. As a scholar and teacher of the written Scriptures He had a full grasp, understanding and insight to each scripture with which we have dealt in this book. He used the common word for wine, *oinos*, as a broad generic term and was more specific when He needed to be.

Christ reveals in His teachings that He had a full understanding of contemporary culture and custom as it related to the care of vineyards, the making of wine and its preservation.

Christ used *"new wine"* as a picture and type of His own teachings, as opposed to the teachings of the Pharisees which was represented by fermented wine (Luke 5:37-39; Mk.2:22; Mt.9:17). During His earthly ministry there were two different drinks called *wine* in Jewish society; one was preserved as an unfermented drink but the other had been carefully taken through the fermentation process to make it intoxicating.

When speaking in Luke 12:45, He spoke as a prophet: He warned that there would be those in the Church in the latter days who would begin to say in their hearts: *"My lord delayeth his coming."* As a result they would begin to *"eat and drink, and to be drunken."* Here we have a prediction that the eating and drinking practices of the world would invade the Church in a marked way just before Jesus Christ would return.

In the next verse we are given the terrible consequence of this: *"The lord of that servant will come in a day when he looketh not for him, and at an hour when he is not aware, and will cut him in sunder, and will appoint him his portion with the unbelievers."*

In Luke 21:34, amidst His teachings concerning the Last Days and His return, He warned of various real practical dangers by which that day could come upon them unawares: *"And take heed to yourselves, lest at any time your hearts be overcharged with surfeiting, and drunkenness, and cares of this life, and so that day come upon you unawares."* The word *"surfeiting"* means to have a headache and for your head to be seized with pain after a time of drinking. This is spoken of alongside *"drunkenness"* but is distinct from it.

We begin to see that the effects of alcohol, social drinking and intoxication will be a very real issue to face the Church just before Jesus returns and that it will bring very serious eternal dangers for many. Many who think themselves followers of Christ who think that they are ready for the sudden catching away of the Church will find that such practices will leave them outside of Christ and under the wrath and judgement of God without remedy.

The Last Supper, Passover & Communion

The very last sermon Christ ever preached to His Disciples was at the Passover. At this last supper, after the meal was finished and the memorial of cup and bread was instituted, Christ taught them in a parable concerning the vine and branches. Christ now reveals Himself as the true vine and His disciples as the branches (Jn.15).

Those who defend the practice of drinking alcohol build upon yet another fundamental myth: they teach that fermented wine was always and only used in the Jewish Passover. By this they infer that there is not a shadow of doubt that Christ and His disciples drank fermented wine. But is this true? **Not once in the Law of Moses is wine spoken of anywhere in connection with the Passover.** What is more surprising is that not once is the word *"wine"* used in connection with the Passover or last supper in the New Testament.

What is clearly stated in the New Testament is that they were to drink from the *"cup"* which Christ gave them which was filled with the *"fruit of the vine"* and which represented the blood of the new covenant (Mt.26:27-29; Mk.14:23-25; Lk.22:17-18; I Cor.11:25-28). It is amazing that Christ, Matthew, Mark, Luke, John and Paul never use the word *"wine"* (*oinos*) even once in connection with the supper or this memorial, which the Church is to keep until Christ returns.

In these scriptures the *fruit of the vine* is mentioned three times and the cup that held it is mentioned ten times. Why did Christ and the apostles not use the word *oinos* (wine)? The term *"fruit of the vine"* expresses what *oinos* does not. *Oinos* is a broad generic term which can mean either fermented or unfermented wine. This word for *"wine"* could have been misunderstood but the term *"fruit of the vine"* clearly explains what Christ wanted to convey. **The drink in the cup which was to represent His blood was pure grape juice.**

It was only in Jewish writings written centuries after the death of Christ that any mention is made concerning fermented wine in connection with the Jewish Passover. As a result of fermented wine being used thus, we read in the very same documents of Rabbis suffering drunkenness and hangovers. This was the inevitable result of Jews using fermented wine instead of the *fruit of the vine* at Passover.

In the Mishna, we are first informed concerning the practice of drinking **four cups** of wine at the Passover meal. Each cup held about three-quarters of a pint which means each person had to drink at least **three pints** of wine during the meal.

If this was the practice at the time of Christ, as many insist, and if the wine was fermented, as again many insist upon, then you can be sure that Christ and His disciples were heavily under the influence of alcohol by the end of the supper.

This of course contradicts all Scriptural teaching on this subject. If such theories and fables were true we can only imagine the state of the Jewish nation at Passover as women, children, the old and the weak are encouraged, taught and commanded that each year they are to drink four cups of fermented wine in remembrance of God's salvation of the nation.

Passover would then become a time to prepare the nation to love intoxication rather than a time to remember their deliverance from the Egyptian captivity. This meal was given in order to stir up their minds to remember, but as we have already seen fermented wine would dull the ability of the mind to think on these things and comprehend them.

We have no problem believing and understanding that unleavened bread was used at the Passover and again that it was used when Christ broke bread and gave it to His disciples as representing His broken body. Unleavened bread was bread that was free from yeast. But why does the church have such a problem believing that the cup which He gave as representing His Blood was free from all ferment?

From John's first pronouncement *"behold the Lamb of God which taketh away the sin of the world"*, we see that Christ was the fulfilment of every lamb that was killed in the Old Testament for sin. The Passover lamb was a type and foreshadow of Christ. Its blood pointed forward to Christ's precious blood.

In fact when Paul writes to the Corinthians he teaches: *"Purge out therefore the old leaven, that ye may be a new lump, as ye are unleavened. For even Christ our passover is sacrificed for us: Therefore let us keep the feast, not with old leaven, neither with the leaven of malice and wickedness; but with the unleavened bread of sincerity and truth"* (I Cor.5:7-8).

In the Old Testament we see clearly that the lamb and its blood was not to be offered with leaven: *"Thou shalt not offer the blood of my sacrifice with leaven; neither shall the sacrifice of the feast of the passover be left unto the morning"* (Ex.34:25). The lamb and the blood which were used at Passover were free from leaven. So also the wine at Passover which represented the blood of the lamb was free from leaven or yeast which meant it was free from the process of fermentation. **The wine Christ**

used at the last supper, in order to fulfil typology, was free from ferment.
Would Christ use an intoxicating drink to represent His precious redeeming blood instead of fresh grape juice? Would He use a drink which Moses warned was *"poison of dragons"* and the *"cruel venom of asps"*, which Solomon said *"biteth like a serpent"* and *"stingeth like an adder"*? Would Christ say *"drink ye all of it"* and contradict Solomon who said, *"Look not thou upon wine when"* it is fermented? Are we to believe that Christ insisted on drinking fermented wine at the Passover and that He then went on to institute it in the public, regular practice of the Church when the Apostles in their later writings utterly forbade its use?

Shortly after the institution of this memorial meal for the church Christ and His Disciples departed to Gethsemane where He sorrowed and prayed in agony of soul to His Heavenly Father that He might be delivered from this cup of suffering. Are we to believe that His mind, emotions and body were under the moderate influence of alcohol in the Garden? Are we to believe that it was affecting the function of His brain and flowing through His veins at the very time Judas arrived with soldiers and betrayed Him with a kiss? Was His head still feeling the effects of more than three pints of wine as He stood in Pilate's judgement hall?

No my friends. Our Saviour was in full, conscious control of all His faculties as He entered these hours of darkness. Prayer would aid Him through this dark trial, not an intoxicating drink which would make Him forget His troubles. Furthermore, if the Disciples had taken three pints of wine at the Passover Christ could have excused them for falling asleep in Gethsemane when He asked them to pray.

Fermented Wine & Calvary's Cross
Let us now look at the last hours Christ passed through on Earth before His death. Christ was offered two different drinks at the time of His crucifixion which were taken from the vine. One He rejected, the other He gladly received. One was intoxicating, the other was refreshing. One was acceptable to God; the other was unacceptable to God.

Both drinks were offered to Christ within a very short time of each other. They were both offered to Christ on mount Calvary (Golgotha the place of the skull). Both were offered by those who stood by. But these two drinks were distinct and different in character, nature and effect.

The first drink was offered to Christ upon His arrival on the mount just before His crucifixion. We are told that *"they gave him to drink wine mingled with myrrh."* This was *oinos* mixed with *"myrrh"* or as Matthew informs us *"mingled with gall."* This gall or myrrh mixture was a bitter drug or poison like poppy or wormwood mixed with strong wine and given to those about to suffer a terrible and prolonged death. The reason of course was that it would stupefy their senses. It would numb their mental, emotional and physical awareness. Solomon said, *"give strong drink to him that is ready to perish"* (Prov.31:6).

But Matthew tells us *"when he had tasted thereof, he would not drink"* and Mark tells us *"but he received it not."* Christ was willing to receive a drink at this time, but refused to drink this intoxicating poison that was offered to Him. He must consciously experience the wrath of God for sinners upon the Cross. He had never drunk fermented wine in life and would not do so in death (Mt.27:33-35; Mk.15:22-24).

He was offered the second drink about three hours later while upon the Cross not long before He died. Before receiving it He said, *"I thirst."* This reveals that the second drink was offered and received in order to help satisfy His thirst—not to numb His senses. *"And straightway one of them ran, and took a spunge, and filled it with vinegar* [oxos], *and put it on a reed, and gave him to drink."* (Mt.27:46-48; Mk.15:34-37; Jn.19:28-30).

All three Gospels state that He was given vinegar (*oxos*) to drink. This *oxos* was also called *posca*. It was the standard official drink of the Roman soldier. It was wine that had gone sour. It was refreshing, satisfying, bitter and free from alcohol. Fermented wine (*oinos*) and vinegar (*oxos*) were both included in soldiers rations but they were distinct drinks. The vinegar was for the soldier on duty and it was a refreshing satisfying drink to aid them in their duties under the hot sun. The fermented wine which they were given was reserved for off-duty. Some Roman

Generals banned fermented wine altogether and only allowed their soldier's *oxos* as a drink because it was free from alcohol and would allow their soldiers to keep their wits about them at all times. This was the drink given to Christ and drunk by Him just before He died.

This fulfilled the Old Testament prophecy: *"They gave me also gall for my meat; and in my thirst they gave me vinegar to drink"* (Ps.69:21). All this was perfectly foretold and then fulfilled. Even in Christ's last rejection of an intoxicating drink and then in partaking of a thirst satisfying drink, He fulfilled all righteousness in providing for us a perfect righteousness to clothe us and a holy example to follow.

One Last Promise
Connected to the fruit of the vine is one last wonderful promise which Christ left us. He said in Matthew: *"But I say unto you, I will not drink henceforth of this fruit of the vine, until that day when I drink it new with you in my Father's kingdom"* (Mt.26:29). Mark says *"in the kingdom of God"* and, Luke says, *"...until the kingdom of God shall come"* (Mk.14:25; Lk.22:18).

As He took that last supper with His disciples and then broke bread and partook of the cup of communion, He left this precious promise which we remember each time we break bread around the Lord's Table on the Lord's Day.

Christ said He would not partake of the fruit of the vine again until we are all with Him. He says that at that time He will *"drink it new"* with us. This will be the literal fruit of the vine but it will be totally new like nothing we have ever had before. It will be fruit of the vine never tasted before. It will not be fermented and it will not be old. It will not be intoxicating and it will not be from Sodom. It will be new, fresh, fruit of the vine which will testify to the work which has been totally completed.

Just as the Disciples sat with Him and drank of the fruit of the vine, so we also shall one day do it literally, physically and visibly. We will no longer take it as a memorial looking back to Calvary or as looking forward to Christ's return but we shall partake of the fruit of the vine as those who have finished their journey and who are now present with their Lord forever. Oh what a day that will be.

But drunkards will not be there: *"nor drunkards...shall inherit the kingdom of God"* (I Cor.6:9). How terrible it shall be for those who loved and embraced their wine bottle or pint of beer or their 'Gin and Tonic', to hear the terrible words, *"I never knew you."* How terrible for those who were addicted to the intoxicating influence of alcohol to know that they are shut out of the kingdom of God for all eternity because they loved it more than Christ. How hopeless, how horrible, how endless shall be their torment.

But how wonderful, how delightful and how eternal shall be the reward of those who have loved Christ, loved His Word, loved holiness and who have embraced the Cross in denying the lusts of the flesh. The sober Blood-washed host of every generation, nation and tongue shall sing *"Worthy is the Lamb that was slain"* as they partake of the cup of blessing filled with the fruit of the vine as they gaze upon their precious Lord Jesus Christ (Rev.5:12). Oh what a day that will be.

*For bulk orders of this book
please contact the author directly.
keithmalcomson@live.co.uk*

SELECT BIBLIOGRAPHY

Books Promoting Abstinence
1. *The Temperance Bible Commentary* by F.R. Lees & D. Burns – 1870, National Temperance Society and Publication House
2. *Christ, the Apostles and Wine* by Dr. Earnest Gordon – 1944, National Women's Christian Temperance Union Publishing House
3. *The Bible and its Wines* by Wesley Ewing D.D. – 1985, The National Prohibition Foundation
4. *Bible Wines or the Laws of Fermentation and the Wines of the Ancients* by William Patton D.D. – 1881, National Temperance Society and Publication House
5. *Scripture Testimony against Intoxicating Wine* by William Ritchie – 1866
6. *The Bible the Saint & the Liquor Industry* by Jim McGuiggan – 1977, International Biblical Resources
7. *Oinos: A Discussion of the Bible Wine Question* by Leon C. Field and H.W. Warren – 1883, Phillips & Hunt
8. *Wine the Biblical Imperative: Total Abstinence* by Robert P. Teachout – 1983

Books Promoting Social-Drinking
1. *Wine in the Bible & the Church* by G.I. Williamson – 1976, Pilgrim Publishing Company
2. *The Wrath of Grapes: Drinking and the Church Divided* by André S. Bustanoby – 1987, Baker Book House Company
3. *God Gave Wine* by Kenneth L. Gentry – 2001, Gentry Family Trust, UDT April
4. *Drinking with Calvin and Luther* by Jim West – 2003, First Oak Edition

5. *Bacchus and Anti-Bacchus* Pt.1 & Pt.2 –April & October 1841, The Princeton Review

Secular Studies
1. *Ancient Wine,* by Patrick E. McGovern – 2007, Princeton University Press
2. *Vine to Bottle: How Wine is Made,* by Simon Woods – 2001, Octopus Publishing Group Limited
3. *Alcohol our Favourite Drug,* by a special committee of the Royal College of Psychiatrists – 1986
4. National Geographic – February 1992
5. *This is Alcohol* by Nick Brownlee – 2002, Sanctuary Publishing Limited

SOBER SAINTS

Printed in Great Britain
by Amazon